YOUR LIFE
IS NOT A
COINCIDENCE

GOD'S HAND

CONSCIOUS DECISIONS

SUBCONSCIOUS INFLUENCE

DISCOVER THE 3 PILLAR PERSPECTIVE THAT WILL TRANSFORM YOUR LIFE!

ALLEN BROWN

Printed in the United States of America
1st Edition November 2024 First Printing

ISBN for paperback: 978-1-964203-02-7
ISBN for eBook: 978-1-964203-03-4

Build Our Kingdom Publishing, LLC. 560 Main St, Stroudsburg, PA 18360

Edited by: Allen Brown

Although the publisher and the author have made every effort to ensure that the information in this book was correct at press time and while this publication is designed to provide accurate information in regard to the subject matter covered, the publisher and the author assume no responsibility for errors, inaccuracies, omissions, or any other inconsistencies herein and hereby disclaim any liability to any party for any loss, damage, or disruption caused by errors or omissions, whether such errors or omissions result from negligence, accident, or any other cause.

This publication is meant as a source of valuable information for the reader, however, it is not meant as a substitute for direct expert assistance. If such a level of assistance is required, the services of a competent professional should be sought.

Scripture References

Scripture quotations marked NIV are taken from the **New International Version® (NIV®)**. Copyright © 1973, 1978, 1984, 2011 by **Biblica, Inc.®** Used by permission. All rights reserved worldwide. For more information, visit www.biblica.com.

Unless otherwise indicated, scripture references are for illustrative purposes and are not tied to a specific Bible translation. Readers are encouraged to consult their preferred version of the Bible.

Table of Contents

Dedication

To the Lord Jesus Christ, the author and finisher of my faith, I dedicate this book with a heart full of gratitude. Your hand has guided me through every chapter of my life, teaching me the lessons that form the foundation of these pages. Thank You for Your unfailing love and divine direction.

To every reader holding this book, I pray these words inspire you to see God's hand in every aspect of your life. May they guide you toward clarity, purpose, and the realization that nothing in your life is a coincidence.

To those who have inspired, challenged, and refined me, thank you for being a part of this journey. Your influence has been a divine tool, shaping me for God's greater purpose.

Acknowledgement

I want to take a moment to acknowledge a young man who has shown support for this book, *Your Life Is Not a Coincidence*. As I was picking up a sample copy from the mail and sharing it with a group of men in the barbershop where my office is located, Jayden DuBose stepped up and became the very first person to purchase this book. Jayden is someone I've had the privilege of mentoring. He attended my barber school and now works in the barbershop, continuing to grow and build his future.

Jayden, I thank you for your encouragement and belief in me and this book. Your support means more than words can express. To everyone reading this, I ask that you send up a prayer for Jayden—that he be blessed, that God's favor guide his path, and that he continues to grow into the man God has called him to be. Jayden, I wish you all the success in the world. May your journey be filled with purpose and fulfillment.

Forward

It's no coincidence that you're reading this book. Regardless of how it came into your hands—whether you heard about it from someone, it was gifted to you, or you stumbled upon it by chance— this moment is intentional. I believe this aligns directly with the **Three Pillar Perspective**, starting with the first pillar: **God's Hand**. This pillar embodies the belief that everything in life happens for a reason, and the fact that you're here, at this exact moment, reading these words, is a reflection of divine timing. God has orchestrated this opportunity for you to access the insights shared within these pages.

As the author, I want you to know that the principles you're about to encounter aren't mere concepts or theories—they're grounded in real-life experience. I have lived these truths, and I can affirm their power with confidence. If you're willing to approach this book with an open heart and mind, you'll discover wisdom that can transform your life. This isn't just about knowledge; it's about applying that knowledge to recognize when God is moving in your life, breaking free from patterns that have held you back, and preventing recurring pain or challenges. By the time you finish this book, you'll have the tools to gain clarity, take control of your journey, and align with your true purpose.

This book is designed to lead you through a transformative process. Many people live their lives without ever discovering the principles that guide fulfillment, leaving them disconnected from their full potential. That won't be your story. Through the wisdom, insights, and tools presented here, you'll uncover how to align your thoughts, actions, and faith with outcomes that reflect your divine purpose. The **Three Pillar Perspective**—God's Hand, Conscious Decisions, and Subconscious Influences—will help you reshape your understanding of life's events, showing you how these forces work together to unlock the life you've always desired.

Everything starts in the mind. Once you grasp the truths shared here, you'll realize how much control you already possess—control that may have been obscured by old habits, assumptions, or fears. This new awareness will empower you to take charge of your life in a way that aligns with your God-given purpose. You'll see how small, intentional shifts in perspective and action can lead to monumental changes in your circumstances.

Before we begin, I want to leave you with this truth: God is your partner. The Bible reminds us that we are co-heirs with Christ, working together with God to fulfill His mission and purpose. Yet, the distractions of the world and the misinformation we've absorbed over time often pull us away from this partnership. Many people live their entire lives unaware of the divine assignment God has placed on their hearts, missing out on the fullness of His plan. That won't be you. This book will reveal timeless wisdom—insights that many never discover—and empower you to step confidently into your purpose, living the life you were created for.

Let's start this journey together. The transformation you've been waiting for begins here.

Romans 8:28

SIGNIFICANCE OF ROMANS 8:28

Before you dive into this book, I want to draw your attention to a scripture that is deeply woven into its message: Romans 8:28. This verse declares, *"And we know that in all things God works for the good of those who love him, who have been called according to his purpose."* It's no coincidence that this scripture appears in these pages eight times, aligning with the three pillars—God's Hand, Conscious Decisions, and Subconscious Influence—that form the foundation of this book.

The reason for emphasizing this scripture is simple: it captures the essence of how these three pillars work together. Just as God orchestrates all things for good, the interplay of these pillars creates the outcomes we experience in life. Romans 8:28 reminds us that nothing is random or wasted; every moment, decision, and influence serves a greater purpose when aligned with His will. The repetition of this verse throughout the book reflects its central role in showing how divine sovereignty, conscious decisions, and subconscious influences combine to shape your life.

As you read, I encourage you to meditate on this truth: all things truly do work together. By understanding how the three pillars align with this divine principle, you'll see how your life's experiences—both good and challenging—can be part of a greater design leading to your purpose and fulfillment.

Introduction
Your Life Is Not a Coincidence

THE QUESTION OF COINCIDENCE

Life often feels like a series of random events—some joyful, some painful, and many that seem to make no sense in the moment. But what if I told you that nothing you've experienced, nothing you've endured, and nothing you've accomplished was ever by chance? What if I told you that every piece of your story, every person who crossed your path, and every obstacle you overcame was all part of a divine design?

This book, *Your Life Is Not a Coincidence,* was written to help you uncover that truth.

A DIVINE ASSIGNMENT

From the moment you came into this world, you've been part of a bigger plan—a divine assignment orchestrated by a God who knew you before you were even born. Just as God told the prophet Jeremiah:

"Before I formed you in the womb I knew you, before you were born I set you apart; I appointed you as a prophet to the nations" **(Jeremiah 1:5).**

So too were you created with intention and purpose.

God didn't just know Jeremiah: He also gave him a purpose and an assignment, appointing him to be a prophet and equipping him with the instructions needed to fulfill his divine role. This process reflects a profound truth: you were not only known by God but also ordained for a specific purpose before you took your first breath.

1

Your life is not random; every circumstance, whether joyful or challenging, is part of the preparation for your assignment.

Like Jeremiah, your assignment may feel overwhelming at times. When God called him, Jeremiah initially protested, saying:

"I do not know how to speak; I am too young" **(Jeremiah 1:6).** Yet God reassured him:

"Do not say, 'I am too young.' You must go to everyone I send you to and say whatever I command you" **(Jeremiah 1:7).**

In the same way, God's plan for you comes with both purpose and provision. He not only sets you apart but also provides the guidance and resources you need to fulfill your unique calling.

You are not an accident. Your circumstances, no matter how chaotic or challenging, are not coincidental. They are purposeful pieces of a larger puzzle designed to bring you closer to the person you are meant to be and the assignment you are meant to fulfill.

THE POWER IN THIS BOOK

This book is more than a collection of ideas or theories; it is my life. This book has been a long time coming, born out of a lifetime of experiences that have shown me how nothing in life is truly random.

I've witnessed firsthand how aligning with God's will, making deliberate choices, and addressing subconscious patterns can produce outcomes that defy explanation. These principles are not abstract ideas—they are proven truths that I've lived, and I'm here to share them with you.

You have more control over your life than you may realize. By understanding how the 3 pillars work together, you'll gain the tools to influence your future, align with divine purpose, and create a life of meaning, fulfillment, and success.

HOW THIS BOOK WILL TRANSFORM YOUR PERSPECTIVE

Throughout this book, I'll share personal stories that illustrate how these 3 pillars—**God's Divine Hand, Conscious Decisions, and Subconscious Influences**—have worked together in my own journey. These stories will show you how specific outcomes—what others might label as coincidences—were deliberate results of God's sovereignty, my intentional decisions, and the subconscious patterns guiding my actions.

Each chapter is structured around four key sections:

1. MY STORY

Every chapter begins with a significant story from my life where all 3 pillars were at work, often in ways that were only clear in hindsight. These stories define how these principles work in action. By sharing my personal journey, I want to bring these concepts to life, showing you how they've worked for me and how they can work for you too.

2. THE 3 PILLARS PERSPECTIVE AT WORK

After sharing my story, I'll break down how each pillar contributed to the result. This section is where we analyze the roles of God's divine intervention, my conscious decisions, and the subconscious influences that shaped the outcome. The goal here is to provide you with clarity on how these forces worked together in my story and to demonstrate how the same principles can apply in your life.

3. A MOMENT TO REFLECT

Reflection is a powerful tool for self-awareness and growth. In this section, I'll ask you specific questions designed to help you reflect on your own journey. These questions will encourage you to identify patterns, actions, and beliefs that have been shaping your results—whether you've realized it or not.

4. TAKE ACTION NOW!

This section is all about taking action. I'll share actionable steps you can take to align with God's divinity, make intentional decisions, and reshape your subconscious mind. These steps are practical tools to help you create outcomes in your life that the world might call coincidences but are, in fact, deliberate results of the pillars working together.

These four sections are designed to guide you through both understanding and application. First, you'll see the principles at work through my story. Then, you'll break down how the pillars created the results, reflect on your own life, and take intentional steps toward shaping your future.

This isn't just a book of ideas—it's a guide to uncovering how your life is shaped and how you can take control of your outcomes. As we journey together, you'll see that nothing in your life has ever been a coincidence. Everything has been working according to a divine plan, and this book is your opportunity to fully step into that truth.

A FINAL ENCOURAGEMENT

As you begin this journey, let me remind you: your life is not a coincidence. Every event, every challenge, and every victory is part of a larger design. This book will help you uncover that design, embrace your role in shaping your future, and fully recognize the power of the 3 pillars at work in your life.

Let's begin this journey together. I'm eager to share my stories, my insights, and this framework with you so that you, too, can recognize that nothing in your life is a coincidence. It's time to take control of your outcomes and live the life you were meant to live.

The 3 Pillar Perspective
Explained

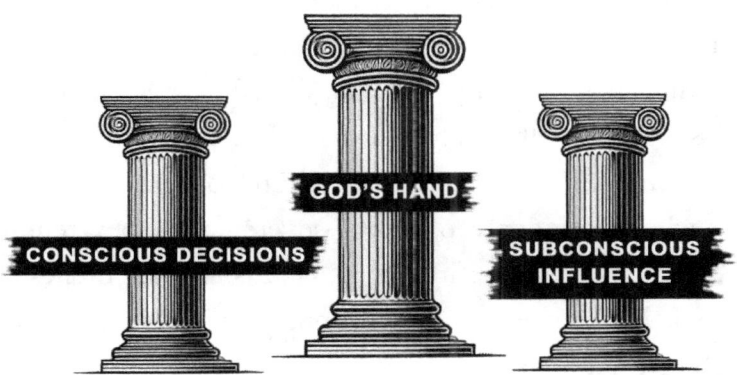

THE 3 PILLARS AT WORK

As I set out to write this book, I searched for a way to help you understand why your life is not a coincidence. I wanted to give you a clear framework to show how every event in your life—good or bad—is connected to a larger design. That's when the concept of the **3 Pillar Perspective** emerged.

These pillars represent the forces at work that shape your experiences and results:

1. **God's Divine Hand**
2. **Conscious Decisions**
3. **Subconscious Influences**

Whether or not you believe in God, these principles operate universally, affecting every life. Together, they create outcomes the world often dismisses as mere coincidences, but as you'll see, nothing could be further from the truth.

PILLAR 1: GOD'S DIVINE HAND

The first pillar, **God's Divine Hand**, is the cornerstone of why your life is not a coincidence. There are moments in your life when events align so perfectly that they defy explanation. These moments—meeting the right person at the right time, narrowly avoiding disaster, or receiving an opportunity you never anticipated—are evidence of God's sovereignty. They remind us that we are not navigating life alone. God is actively orchestrating events, placing people in our paths, and guiding circumstances to fulfill His greater plan.

Think about Joseph from the Bible. Sold into slavery by his brothers, falsely accused, and imprisoned, Joseph could have easily viewed his life as a series of unfortunate coincidences. But in Genesis 50:20, he tells his brothers:

"You intended to harm me, but God intended it for good to accomplish what is now being done, the saving of many lives."

What seemed like unrelated hardships were all part of God's plan to position Joseph for a greater purpose.

THE EIGHT CHARACTERISTICS OF GOD'S DIVINE HAND

God's Divine Hand works through eight characteristics that reveal His sovereignty:

1. **Divinity:** The supernatural alignment of events that could only be orchestrated by God.
2. **Sovereignty:** God's absolute control over all circumstances.

3. **Favor:** Unearned blessings that position you for success.
4. **Protection:** Moments when God shields you from harm, often without you realizing it.
5. **Provision:** Resources and opportunities that come when you need them most.
6. **Guidance:** God's direction through circumstances, people, or inner conviction.
7. **Intervention:** When God steps in to change the course of events for His purpose.
8. **Timing:** The perfection of when and how events unfold in your life.

EXAMPLES OF GOD'S DIVINE HAND

Example 1: A Life-Saving Delay

Have you ever been delayed unexpectedly—missing a bus or taking a detour—only to find out later that the delay kept you from harm? That's no coincidence; it's God's Protection and Timing working together to safeguard you.

Example 2: A Timely Introduction

Imagine meeting someone seemingly by chance, only to discover later that they had the resources, wisdom, or connection you desperately needed. That's God's Divinity and Favor aligning circumstances for His greater purpose.

PILLAR 2: CONSCIOUS DECISIONS

The second pillar is **Conscious Decisions**—the deliberate choices you make every day that lead to specific results. Whether you believe in God or not, this principle applies universally: your life is shaped by the seeds you sow through your actions.

The Bible puts it plainly in Galatians 6:7:

"A man reaps what he sows."

Every decision you make—whether driven by intention, desire, or belief—sets events into motion that create outcomes that are no coincidence.

THE EIGHT PRINCIPLES OF CONSCIOUS DECISIONS

Conscious Decisions operate through eight key principles:

1. **Intentionality:** Making deliberate decisions to achieve specific outcomes.
2. **Discipline:** Consistently aligning your actions with your goals.
3. **Risk:** Taking bold steps that push you beyond your comfort zone.
4. **Responsibility:** Owning the consequences of your decisions.
5. **Preparation:** Laying the groundwork for success.
6. **Adaptability:** Adjusting to challenges while staying focused on your goals.
7. **Focus:** Maintaining clarity and direction in your actions.
8. **Accountability:** Measuring your progress and holding yourself responsible.

EXAMPLES OF CONSCIOUS DECISIONS

Example 1: Pursuing Wealth

A person who spends years studying investment strategies, seeking mentorship, and taking calculated financial risks might eventually achieve financial success. Their wealth isn't random; it's the product of **Preparation, Discipline, and Focus**.

Example 2: A Wrong Choice

Someone who consciously decides to commit a crime may face imprisonment or diminished trust. The consequences aren't coincidental; they're the inevitable result of their **Intentionality and Responsibility (or lack thereof).**

PILLAR 3: SUBCONSCIOUS INFLUENCES

The third pillar, **Subconscious Influences**, is the most subtle yet equally powerful force at work in your life. Your subconscious mind stores habits, beliefs, and patterns that shape your decisions, often without your conscious awareness. These influences, whether positive or negative, impact your actions and results in ways that are far from coincidental.

THE EIGHT ELEMENTS OF SUBCONSCIOUS INFLUENCES

Subconscious influences are shaped by eight core elements:

1. **Beliefs:** Deeply held convictions that drive behavior.
2. **Habits:** Repeated actions that form patterns in your life.
3. **Fears:** Subconscious anxieties that influence your decisions.
4. **Biases:** Unseen preferences or judgments that shape perception.
5. **Memories:** Past experiences that inform your current responses.
6. **Assumptions:** Conclusions drawn without full awareness or facts.
7. **Motivations:** Hidden drivers behind your actions.
8. **Expectations:** What you anticipate, often shaping the outcome.

EXAMPLES OF SUBCONSCIOUS INFLUENCES

Example 1: Financial Struggles

Someone raised to believe that "money is the root of all evil" may subconsciously sabotage opportunities for financial success, creating a cycle of struggle that feels inevitable.

Example 2: Positive Programming Leads to Resilience

A person raised in an environment emphasizing perseverance and self-belief may naturally adapt to challenges with resilience, creating opportunities for success.

BRINGING THE PILLARS TOGETHER

The 3 Pillars—**God's Divine Hand, Conscious Decisions, and Subconscious Influences**—are not isolated forces working in your life. They are deeply interconnected, shaping the outcomes you experience daily.

What the world often calls coincidences are, in truth, the intricate workings of these pillars shaping your story. As you continue this journey, you'll see how each pillar contributes uniquely to your results, and you'll learn how to align them for maximum impact.

Chapter 1
The Place You Were Born
Is No Coincidence

A DIVINE SETUP

My Story #1: I was born in Brooklyn, New York, to two loving parents who became the vessels through which God introduced me to this world. Even at that stage, there was divine intent in where I was born and the family I was placed into. My parents later moved us to Queens, New York, a diverse neighborhood filled with people from all different backgrounds—Indian, German, Asian, Italian, West Indian, Hispanic, African American, and more. Growing up in this environment shaped my worldview in ways I couldn't have understood at the time.

While many of my peers faced cultural divides or racial challenges, my childhood was marked by harmony. My friends and I joked about our differences but never let them separate us. This gave me a unique perspective early on: I learned to see people beyond their labels, to value their humanity. That wasn't a coincidence. God placed me there intentionally to mold a mindset in me that would later be essential in my life and career.

Even the small details mattered. My parents' values and the love they showed me created a foundation that allowed me to thrive. Their stories of overcoming struggles in their own time gave me a sense of resilience and purpose. Everything—the move to Queens, the diversity, the lack of certain hardships that others experienced— was part of God's divine setup to prepare me for my assignment.

One memory that stands out is how my parents worked tirelessly to provide for us. They didn't just teach me the value of hard work—they modeled it daily. My father would often share stories about his own upbringing, highlighting the importance of integrity, perseverance, and faith. My mother, on the other hand, had an innate ability to create a nurturing environment that felt safe and loving, even when times were tough. These foundational lessons were all part of God's plan to prepare me for the journey ahead.

YOUR STORY: REFLECTING ON YOUR BEGINNINGS

Now, take a moment to reflect on your own life.

- Where were you born?
- What was your family like?
- What were the circumstances surrounding your childhood?

Maybe you were born into wealth, or perhaps you faced poverty. Maybe your parents were loving, or maybe you grew up without them. Whatever your circumstances, they were not accidental.

You may find yourself questioning why you were born into a specific situation. *"Why this family?" "Why this town?" "Why this struggle?"* But what if, instead of asking "why," you asked "what?"—What is God trying to show me through this? What did I gain from this environment? Whether it was privilege or pain, every part of your upbringing contributed to the person you are today.

For example:

If you were born into a difficult family situation, maybe God was cultivating resilience, independence, or compassion in you.

If you grew up with abundance, perhaps it was to teach you how to steward resources wisely or share them with others.

Even the geographical location of your birth has significance. God knew the culture, challenges, and opportunities that would surround you, and He chose that place for a reason.

THE 3 PILLAR PERSPECTIVE AT WORK

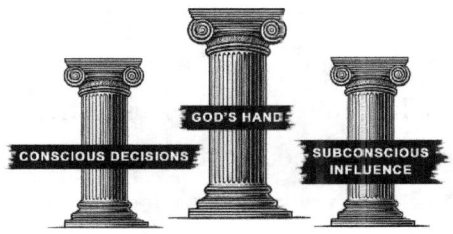

Pillar 1 - God's Divine Hand

God's hand was unmistakably present in every aspect of my beginnings, and it's crucial to recognize how His divine orchestration sets the stage for our lives. My birth in Brooklyn and subsequent upbringing in Queens were not just geographic happenstances but intentional placements designed by God. The multicultural environment of Queens wasn't merely a backdrop—it was a divine classroom. Each friendship and interaction taught me values that would become foundational to my purpose, all under God's guidance.

It's important to understand that God doesn't operate in randomness. What may seem like ordinary circumstances to the world are actually purposeful steps in a larger design. Nothing about my upbringing was coincidental; it was a deliberate act of God to prepare me for a life of inclusivity, leadership, and empathy. Reflect on your own beginnings. Do you see how God's hand has been quietly at work, positioning you for something greater?

Pillar 2 - Conscious Decisions

While God orchestrates the bigger picture, our conscious decisions play a critical role in aligning with His plan. My parents' deliberate choice to move us from Brooklyn to Queens was a pivotal decision that influenced the trajectory of my life. Their actions were intentional, seeking a better environment for me, and they sowed seeds of resilience, adaptability, and a broader worldview.

As I grew older, my own choices reflected these values. Choosing to engage with people from different cultures, to see humanity beyond stereotypes, and to lean into the principles my parents instilled were all conscious decisions that aligned with the life God was calling me to live. These decisions were not coincidental—they were part of a chain of actions leading to a purpose far greater than I could have understood at the time. What intentional steps can you take today to align with the path God is laying out for you?

Pillar 3 - Subconscious Influences

Subconsciously, the environment we live in and the values we absorb shape us in ways we don't always notice. Growing up in a culturally diverse neighborhood wasn't something I thought deeply about as a child, but it was influencing how I viewed the world. It wasn't a coincidence that God placed me in an environment that would teach me to embrace differences and approach others with kindness and understanding. These lessons, planted in my subconscious, became habits and instincts that shaped my actions without deliberate effort.

We often underestimate how much our subconscious patterns are shaped by the seeds God plants along the way. The way I naturally connected with people from all walks of life wasn't just a personality trait—it was a result of the environment God intentionally placed me in. This is why it's so important to reflect on the subtle ways God is shaping you even when you're unaware.

INSIGHTFUL WISDOM

- **Your Family Is Part of the Plan:** Whether your family was a source of love or pain, they were chosen by God as part of your divine setup.
- **Your Environment Shapes You:** The community, culture, and even the time period you were born into are all intentional.
- **God's Purpose Is Bigger Than Your Circumstances:** Every detail, from your parents' decisions to the place you called home, has a role in your story.
- **Reflect on the Lessons:** Look back at your early years and ask yourself: *What did this teach me? How did this prepare me for where I am now?*

A MOMENT TO REFLECT

Write down some of the key elements of your own story:
- Who were the most influential people in your early life?
- What challenges or privileges shaped you?
- How have those things impacted the person you've become today?

CHAPTER CONCLUSION: EMBRACE YOUR ORIGIN STORY

No matter where you were born or what circumstances surrounded your arrival in this world, it was no accident. Just as God told Jeremiah, He knew you before you were formed in the womb.

He chose your family, your neighborhood, and your environment for a reason. Every detail was part of a divine setup to shape you into the person you are meant to be.

Understanding that your birthplace is no coincidence sets the stage for uncovering how every aspect of your life—past and present—is part of God's grand design. This foundation helps you recognize that nothing about your journey has been random or wasted. Where you started is just the beginning of the divine masterpiece God is creating through your life.

TAKE ACTION NOW!

1. PRAY FOR UNDERSTANDING OF YOUR BEGINNINGS

Why: If you pray and ask God to show you how the circumstances of your birth were part of His plan, you will begin to see the divine purpose in your origins.

Result: This understanding will help you find clarity and peace, knowing that every detail of your life is intentional.

Scripture Reference: *"In all your ways submit to him, and he will make your paths straight."* (Proverbs 3:6)

2. RECOGNIZE GOD'S SOVEREIGNTY OVER YOUR BIRTHPLACE

Why: When you acknowledge that God chose your family, culture, and environment for a reason, you will better appreciate the unique opportunities and challenges they brought.

Result: This recognition helps you trust that God has positioned you perfectly for the assignment He has planned for you.

Scripture Reference: *"The boundary lines have fallen for me in pleasant places; surely I have a delightful inheritance."* (Psalm 16:6)

3. HONOR THE ROLE OF YOUR PARENTS

Why: When you express gratitude to your parents or guardians for the values they instilled in you, you align yourself with God's command to honor them.

Result: This action brings healing to your heart and strengthens your ability to see God's work in your upbringing, even in difficult relationships.

Scripture Reference: *"Honor your father and your mother, so that you may live long in the land the Lord your God is giving you."* (Exodus 20:12)

4. COMMIT TO LIVING WITH INTENTIONALITY

Why: When you take deliberate steps to align your actions with the values you've learned, you actively participate in shaping your future.

Result: Your intentional efforts will lead to growth, clarity, and a life that reflects God's purpose for you.

Scripture Reference: *"Whatever you do, work at it with all your heart, as working for the Lord, not for human masters."* (Colossians 3:23)

5. REMOVE BIAS FROM YOUR MINDSET

Why: By intentionally seeing others through God's love and treating them with dignity, you break down barriers of prejudice and reflect Christ's character.

Result: This practice opens doors for meaningful relationships and fosters unity in the environments God has placed you in.

Scripture Reference: *"There is neither Jew nor Gentile, neither slave nor free, nor is there male and female, for you are all one in Christ Jesus."* (Galatians 3:28)

6. SEEK WISDOM THROUGH SCRIPTURE

Why: Spending time in God's Word helps you understand how He uses environments and circumstances to shape His people.

Result: As you learn from biblical examples, you gain insight and direction for navigating your own life.

Scripture Reference: *"For the Lord gives wisdom; from his mouth come knowledge and understanding."* (Proverbs 2:6)

7. IDENTIFY A STEP YOU CAN TAKE TODAY TOWARD THE PURPOSE GOD HAS FOR YOU

Why: Taking small, intentional steps toward your God-given purpose aligns you with His divine plan and opens the door to greater opportunities.

Result: Each step of faith brings you closer to fulfilling the assignment He created you for, just as embracing diversity in my neighborhood taught me to see beyond labels.

Scripture Reference: *"For we are God's handiwork, created in Christ Jesus to do good works, which God prepared in advance for us to do."* (Ephesians 2:10)

Chapter 2
The Neighborhood
That Shaped You

A DIVINE SETUP IN QUEENS

My Story #2: Every neighborhood carries its own character—its own rhythm of life that shapes the people within it. Growing up in Queens, New York, wasn't just an address or a backdrop to my childhood; it was a masterclass in diversity, community, and understanding the power of connection. Queens wasn't just a melting pot of cultures—it was a mosaic, with each piece offering something unique. The lessons I learned from this environment went far beyond appreciating differences; they prepared me to navigate the complexities of relationships, leadership, and faith with wisdom and empathy.

Queens wasn't only about diversity—it was about coexistence. I wasn't just surrounded by people of different ethnicities and backgrounds; I shared meals with them, played on the same streets, and learned to see the world through their eyes. Those early years taught me that God doesn't just work within one culture, language, or belief system. He weaves His purpose through all people, using their unique experiences to teach us lessons we couldn't learn on our own.

One vivid memory I carry is walking to the corner store, passing homes that each told a different story: the vibrant smells of West Indian spices, the colorful festivals of my Hispanic neighbors, and the meticulous gardens of my Italian friends. Each interaction brought a deeper understanding of humanity and helped me develop a skill I didn't recognize at the time—an ability to connect with anyone, no matter their background. I see now that God was planting seeds of adaptability, compassion, and a global perspective long before I understood how essential those traits would become.

THE ROLE OF YOUR ENVIRONMENT

Your environment shapes your perspective in profound ways. For me, growing up in a diverse neighborhood allowed me to see people as individuals rather than stereotypes. While some of my friends who lived in racially homogenous neighborhoods grew up with biases or fears about people who were different, I didn't. My environment taught me that diversity was a strength, not a threat.

This early exposure to different cultures also helped me develop empathy and adaptability—qualities that became invaluable in my personal and professional life. I could walk into any room, connect with people from all walks of life, and find common ground. That wasn't just luck; it was the result of the environment God placed me in.

A LESSON IN OPPORTUNITIES

One of the key things I took away from my neighborhood was the importance of opportunity. Because of where I lived, I had access to programs and experiences that weren't available everywhere. For example, my older cousin introduced me to the Boy Scouts, a program that profoundly influenced my development. Our troop was incredibly diverse, which was unusual for many Boy Scout groups at the time. This diversity gave me even more time to interact with people from different backgrounds, broadening my understanding of the world.

The Boy Scouts didn't just teach me practical skills; they gave me opportunities to lead, even before I thought I was ready. When I was around 13 years old, I was asked to become an assistant patrol leader for a newly formed patrol in my troop. At the time, I had no idea what the role entailed or whether I was capable of handling it. But I said yes, and that decision marked the beginning of my journey as a leader.

STEPPING INTO LEADERSHIP

I'll never forget that first Jamboree. As soon as we arrived, Eric, the patrol leader, turned to me and asked, "What should we do?" I didn't know where my response came from, but I instinctively said, "Let's find out what's required for us to win." I told him to get the judging sheet, which listed all the criteria for the competition. The sheet had about 30 items, rated on a scale from 1 to 5, and we would be judged three times a day.

I took the sheet and began systematically checking off tasks. I inspected our campsite, made sure everyone's uniforms were neat, and ensured our food preparation met the highest standards. I wasn't trying to be in charge, but something inside me told me to take responsibility. When the judges came around, we were ready.

To my surprise, we won the competition. Out of a few hundred scouts, our patrol, the Flaming Arrows, took first place. When they called our name, I was in shock. But what shocked me even more was that I didn't receive any recognition. The celebration went to the patrol leader, Eric, who stood in front of everyone and accepted the award.

At first, I felt a twinge of disappointment. But as I reflected on the experience, I realized that God was teaching me a valuable lesson: **leadership isn't about recognition; it's about serving**

others. That moment shaped my character in ways I couldn't have predicted.

THE 3 PILLAR PERSPECTIVE AT WORK

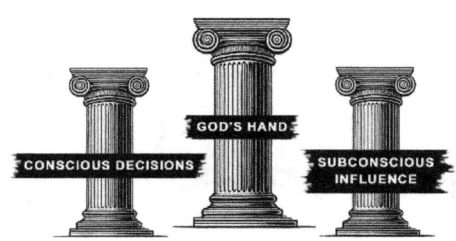

Pillar 1 - God's Divine Hand

God's hand wasn't just present in placing me in Queens—it was evident in how He used the environment to create opportunities that expanded my perspective, (**favor, timing**). The rich diversity of Queens taught me more than just tolerance; it taught me the beauty of collaboration, (**sovereignty**). Each culture I encountered revealed unique ways of thinking, problem-solving, and approaching life, lessons that would later help me connect with people across boundaries in ways I couldn't have predicted.

Even the Boy Scouts wasn't just about leadership or earning merit badges—it was about learning how to lead a team of individuals with different strengths and personalities, (**provision**). That formative experience, orchestrated by God, equipped me to lead diverse groups in business and ministry later in life.

Pillar 2 - Conscious Decisions

While God placed me in an environment rich with lessons, the decisions I made within that environment were equally important. Saying "yes" to joining the Boy Scouts was a pivotal conscious decision, (**risk, intentionality**). I could have resisted the opportunity or dismissed it, but instead, I chose to step into an unknown space and embrace the lessons it offered.

Another significant conscious decision was my willingness to form genuine connections with people who were different from me, (**adaptability**). In a neighborhood as diverse as Queens, I could have stayed within my comfort zone and associated only with those who looked like me. Instead, I chose to see people as individuals rather than labels, (**focus, discipline**). That mindset became a cornerstone of my personal and professional life.

Pillar 3 - Subconscious Influences

Growing up in Queens, my subconscious instincts were shaped by the unique rhythm of the community, (**habits, biases**). The neighborhood taught me to adapt quickly, to approach differences with curiosity rather than judgment, and to find common ground even in unfamiliar situations, (**beliefs**).

My subconscious also absorbed resilience from my parents' example, (**memories**). They worked hard, navigated challenges with grace, and showed me what it meant to persevere. Without being fully aware of it at the time, their actions instilled in me a belief that no obstacle was too great to overcome, (**motivations**).

INSIGHTFUL WISDOM

Your Environment Shapes Your Mindset: The people and experiences in your neighborhood contribute to how you see the world.

Opportunities Are Often Hidden: Sometimes, the things we take for granted are divine gifts waiting to be recognized.

Leadership Starts Early: Your environment likely gave you opportunities to lead, serve, or grow.

> **God's Placement Is Intentional:** Where you were placed wasn't random.

A MOMENT TO REFLECT

Take a moment to write down your thoughts about your neighborhood:

- What were the defining features of your environment?
- Who were the key people who influenced you?
- What opportunities or challenges did you encounter?
- How do you think your environment shaped the person you are today?

CHAPTER CONCLUSION: IT'S NOT A COINCIDENCE

The neighborhood you grew up in wasn't just a backdrop for your childhood; it was a classroom for life. Every interaction, every opportunity, and every challenge played a role in shaping who you are today. Even if your environment felt limiting or difficult, it was part of a divine plan to prepare you for your purpose.

As you reflect on your own story, I hope you begin to see the divine hand in every detail. It wasn't a coincidence. You were placed exactly where you needed to be to become the person God designed you to be.

TAKE ACTION NOW!

1. PRAY FOR CLARITY AND GRATITUDE

Why: If you pray and ask God to reveal how your neighborhood shaped you, you will gain clarity about the lessons and opportunities He placed there. Gratitude for your environment opens your heart to see His divine orchestration more clearly.

Result: You'll begin to appreciate the unique ways God used your surroundings to prepare you for your purpose, even in challenging circumstances.

Scripture Reference: *"Give thanks in all circumstances; for this is God's will for you in Christ Jesus."* (1 Thessalonians 5:18)

2. RECOGNIZE THE OPPORTUNITIES AROUND YOU

Why: When you intentionally reflect on your current environment, you'll discover resources, relationships, and programs that are often overlooked. Recognizing these opportunities is a step toward embracing God's provision.

Result: By engaging with the opportunities God has placed around you, you'll grow and strengthen your skills for His purpose.

Scripture Reference: *"Make the most of every opportunity, because the days are evil."* (Ephesians 5:16)

3. ENGAGE WITH PEOPLE OUTSIDE YOUR COMFORT ZONE

Why: When you step out of your comfort zone to connect with people from different backgrounds, you reflect God's love and expand your ability to relate to others. This deepens your empathy and builds valuable relationships.

Result: You'll develop the ability to navigate diverse environments with grace, opening doors to meaningful connections and greater opportunities.

Scripture Reference: *"Carry each other's burdens, and in this way you will fulfill the law of Christ."* (Galatians 6:2)

4. LEAD WITH HUMILITY

Why: If you step into leadership with humility, you allow God to guide you and teach you to serve others selflessly. This approach aligns your leadership with God's character.

Result: You'll grow into a leader who inspires trust and collaboration, creating lasting impact wherever you serve.

Scripture Reference: *"Humble yourselves before the Lord, and he will lift you up."* (James 4:10)

5. IDENTIFY HIDDEN GEMS IN YOUR SURROUNDINGS

Why: When you take the time to reflect on the "hidden gems" in your environment—resources, mentors, or experiences—you uncover God's provision for your growth.

Result: By recognizing and embracing these gems, you'll strengthen your abilities and gain confidence to pursue the path God has set for you.

Scripture Reference: *"You will seek me and find me when you seek me with all your heart."* (Jeremiah 29:13)

6. TAKE A STEP OF FAITH

Why: When you take a step of faith to engage more deeply with your environment, you align your actions with God's purpose. This act of trust allows Him to open doors for your growth.

Result: By stepping out in faith, you'll discover new opportunities and experience God's provision in ways you never imagined.

Scripture Reference: *"Trust in the Lord with all your heart and lean not on your own understanding."* (Proverbs 3:5)

7. REFLECT ON THE LESSONS FROM YOUR NEIGHBORHOOD

Why: When you reflect on the lessons your neighborhood taught you, you'll uncover the ways God used your environment to shape your character and prepare you for the future.

Result: These reflections will help you understand how to use those lessons in your current season and future endeavors.

Scripture Reference: *"We know that in all things God works for the good of those who love him, who have been called according to his purpose."* (Romans 8:28)

8. BE A POSITIVE INFLUENCE IN YOUR COMMUNITY

Why: By choosing to be a light in your environment, you demonstrate God's love and inspire those around you to see His work through your actions.

Result: Your presence and actions will bless others, creating a ripple effect that glorifies God and strengthens your community.

Scripture Reference: *"In the same way, let your light shine before others, that they may see your good deeds and glorify your Father in heaven."* (Matthew 5:16)

Chapter 3
The Gift of Talent—No Coincidence

A DIVINE SETUP

My Story #3: When I look at the miraculous things God has done in my life through the gift of music, I'm still in awe. If I didn't have the insights I now have, I might have dismissed my journey as a series of coincidences. But knowing what I know today, I recognize that none of it was by chance. Every step of my journey, from the first piano I touched to the global music platforms I've built, was part of God's divine plan.

Today, I've been blessed to create platforms that have helped thousands of producers generate millions of dollars. These platforms not only provide financial stability for others but have also allowed me to take care of my family and live in financial freedom. Music opened those doors for me. But to fully understand how I got here, we need to go back to the beginning—to moments that seemed random but were actually part of God's perfect setup.

THE SEED OF MUSIC: A FIFTH-GRADE TEST

I vividly remember the day in fifth grade when my classmates and I were called into the school auditorium. None of us knew what was about to happen. A teacher stood at the front by a piano, joined by another instructor. After we recited the Pledge of Allegiance and sang the school song, the teacher explained that we'd be taking a test to see if we were musically inclined.

At the time, I didn't think much of it. But as I stood in line waiting for my turn, something inside me stirred—a faint connection to the piano I had spent hours playing at my uncle A.D.'s house in Virginia. During visits to his home, while my cousins played outside or upstairs, I often found myself drawn to his piano. Even though I didn't know how to play, I would sit there, tapping out little tunes that sounded good to me. I didn't understand it at the time, but this was one of my first exposures to music, and God was planting seeds early.

When my turn came during the fifth-grade test, the teacher played a note on the piano and asked me to hum it back. I did. She played another, and I matched it. This continued for several notes, and when I was finished, she marked something on her paper and called the next student. I didn't think much about it until a few days later when I was called into a separate room.

"You passed the music test," the teacher told me. "You were able to recognize and mimic the notes, which means you have a natural musical ability. Now you have the opportunity to join either the band or the orchestra."

At the time, I knew I didn't want to play a string instrument like my sister, who was a violinist. But the band—with its trumpets, trombones, and drums—excited me. I chose the trumpet, a decision that would change my life. That one test, which might seem like a random occurrence, was the first step in a divine plan that would unfold over decades.

FROM BAND TO BAYSIDE: DOORS OPEN THROUGH MUSIC

Joining the band became a journey that lasted through high school. I not only learned to play the trumpet but also developed a deep understanding of music theory, which would prove invaluable later in life. I eventually graduated from Bayside High School in New York with a music theory diploma.

Bayside wasn't even in my school district. To attend, I had to audition, and the only way to get in was through music or art. Interestingly, what originally drew me to Bayside was its reputation for having one of the best football programs in the area. But music—not football—became my entry point. Looking back, it's clear that even this was orchestrated by God. Music opened doors that would have otherwise been closed to me.

FROM MUSIC TO BUSINESS: A NEW CHAPTER

After high school, I didn't immediately pursue music professionally. But a few years after, I was drawn to music production. My early training in music gave me a foundation to excel, and I eventually opened a music studio in Queens in my early twenties after completing audio engineering school. That studio became a hub for local artists, and I helped many of them create and produce their music. I was proud of what I was building, but there came a time when I felt called to shift my focus.

In my early twenties, I shut down my studio and donated my equipment. I had recently given my life to Christ and was committed to pursuing spiritual growth. At the time, I didn't know how everything would come together, but I trusted that God had a plan.

THE MILLION DOLLAR SEED: ACTS OF FAITH

This phase of my life is detailed in my first book, **Million Dollar Seed.** If you haven't read it, the book explains how I gave everything away to pursue what God had for me. It wasn't about asking for money; it was about asking for direction and trusting that God would provide.

In the process, God supernaturally connected me with Grammy Award-winning producer Rockwilder. At the time, I had no idea how significant this connection would be. We collaborated on a website for music producers—a platform that would go on to generate millions of dollars for producers around the world. This platform became the financial breakthrough I had prayed for, providing not only for my family but also for my ability to pursue other ventures and passions.

If you're interested in the full story, I encourage you to read my first book **Million Dollar Seed.** But for now, I want to focus on the larger point: none of this was coincidental. Every step—from the piano at my uncle's house to the band in fifth grade to the connection with Rockwilder—was orchestrated by God.

THE 3 PILLAR PERSPECTIVE AT WORK

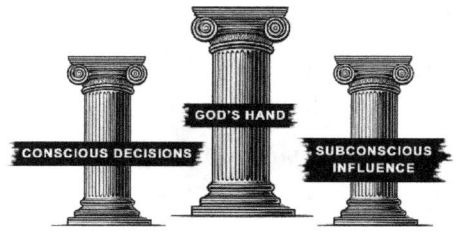

Pillar 1 - God's Divine Hand

God's hand was undeniably present in the moments that revealed my musical gift. The seemingly routine music test in fifth grade wasn't just a random school activity—it was a divine appointment. **(timing).** From the early days of playing my uncle's piano to being chosen for the band based on that test, God was planting seeds and guiding me toward a path that would define my life's work, **(favor, provision).**

Even the audition for Bayside High School, which wasn't in my district, was more than just a logistical hurdle. It was a divine opening that set me on a trajectory toward deeper musical understanding and opportunities I couldn't have imagined. **(sovereignty).** Reflect on your own journey—what "small" moments or seemingly ordinary opportunities have revealed themselves as clear signs of God moving in your life?

Pillar 2 - Conscious Decisions

My decision to pursue music seriously, from selecting the trumpet over other instruments to taking the Bayside audition, were intentional steps that aligned with the opportunities God was opening for me. **(intentionality, discipline).** These actions required commitment, effort, and a willingness to step outside my comfort zone. While God provides the direction, our actions determine how we walk the path He has laid before us.

Later, my decision to open a music studio was another conscious choice rooted in faith and ambition, **(risk).** By stepping into music production, I wasn't just following a passion—I was leaning into a divine plan that would later supernaturally connect me with influential figures like Grammy-winning producer Rockwilder, **(focus, preparation).** What intentional actions are you taking to step into the purpose God has revealed for you?

Pillar 3 - Subconscious Influences

The influence of my childhood experiences with music ran deeper than I realized at the time, **(beliefs, habits).** Subconsciously, the time I spent exploring my uncle's piano shaped a natural inclination toward music long before I ever recognized it as a talent.

It was God working quietly, embedding a love and curiosity for music in me that would later become the foundation for my career and ministry.

Even my openness to exploring music production and business was influenced by habits and thought patterns that had been developing since childhood, **(motivations)**. Without fully realizing it, my subconscious drive to create, innovate, and explore new avenues was already aligning me with the opportunities God would later provide.

INSIGHTFUL WISDOM

- **God Plants Seeds Early:** Your childhood interests and natural inclinations weren't random. They were intentional gifts from God to prepare you for your purpose.
- **Opportunities Are Divine Setups:** The unexpected events or opportunities in your life—whether it's a school program, a mentor, or an unforeseen path—are part of God's intricate plan.
- **Faith Unlocks Potential:** When you trust God and align your talents with His purpose, He will open doors you couldn't have imagined.
- **Your Talents Are Tools for Impact:** Your skills and passions aren't just for personal fulfillment. They're meant to bless others and glorify God.

A MOMENT TO REFLECT

- What were your natural interests or talents as a child?

- Were there moments or opportunities that appeared ordinary but later revealed themselves as pivotal in shaping your path?
- How have your talents guided your life and purpose so far?
- What steps can you take to align your gifts with God's plan for your life?

CHAPTER CONCLUSION: IT'S NOT A COINCIDENCE

Looking back on my life, it's clear that every step was guided by God. The piano at my uncle's house, the fifth-grade music test, the high school band, the studio, and even meeting Rockwilder—none of it was random. Every moment was part of a divine plan to position me where I needed to be.

The same is true for you. Your talents, opportunities, and experiences are all part of God's design. Embrace them, trust His timing, and remember it's not a coincidence.

TAKE ACTION NOW!

1. PRAY FOR CLARITY AND DIRECTION

Why: When you ask God to reveal your talents and guide your steps, He will give you wisdom to recognize opportunities.

Result: Clarity about your gifts and confidence in pursuing them.

Scripture Reference: *"If any of you lacks wisdom, you should ask God, who gives generously to all without finding fault, and it will be given to you."* (James 1:5)

2. REFLECT ON YOUR CHILDHOOD INTERESTS

Why: Your childhood passions often reveal the seeds God planted in you.

Result: A deeper understanding of how your early interests align with God's purpose for your life.

Scripture Reference: *"For we are God's handiwork, created in Christ Jesus to do good works, which God prepared in advance for us to do."* (Ephesians 2:10)

3. TAKE ACTION ON AN OPPORTUNITY IN FRONT OF YOU

Why: Acting on opportunities opens doors that align with God's plan.

Result: Progress and growth in using your gifts to glorify Him.

Scripture Reference: *"Whatever you do, work at it with all your heart, as working for the Lord, not for human masters."* (Colossians 3:23)

4. INVEST TIME IN LEARNING

Why: Honing your skills equips you to maximize your potential.

Result: Increased opportunities and preparedness for what God has in store.

Scripture Reference: *"Do your best to present yourself to God as one approved, a worker who does not need to be ashamed and who correctly handles the word of truth."* (2 Timothy 2:15)

5. ALIGN YOUR TALENTS WITH SERVICE

Why: Using your gifts to bless others reflects God's love.

Result: Fulfillment and impact beyond yourself.

Scripture Reference: *"Each of you should use whatever gift you have received to serve others, as faithful stewards of God's grace in its various forms."* (1 Peter 4:10)

6. CONNECT WITH MENTORS OR LIKE-MINDED INDIVIDUALS

Why: Relationships are a key part of God's plan to grow you.

Result: Growth through collaboration and shared wisdom.

Scripture Reference: *"Plans fail for lack of counsel, but with many advisers they succeed."* (Proverbs 15:22)

7. TRUST IN GOD'S TIMING

Why: His plan unfolds in His perfect time.

Result: Peace and assurance as you move forward in faith.

Scripture Reference: *"There is a time for everything, and a season for every activity under the heavens."* (Ecclesiastes 3:1)

8. SURRENDER YOUR PLAN TO GOD

Why: Trusting Him allows His purpose to prevail over your own.

Result: Alignment with God's perfect will.

Scripture Reference: *"Many are the plans in a person's heart, but it is the Lord's purpose that prevails."* (Proverbs 19:21)

9. CELEBRATE SMALL WINS

Why: Acknowledging progress, no matter how small, builds faith and keeps you moving forward.

Result: Encouragement and momentum to continue trusting God's process.

Scripture Reference: *"Do not despise these small beginnings, for the Lord rejoices to see the work begin."* (Zechariah 4:10)

Chapter 4
The Power of Independence and Recognizing Divine Guidance

A DIVINE SEED OF INDEPENDENCE

My Story #4: In the previous chapter, I shared how music became a pathway to financial freedom and a fulfilling life. But as rewarding as my journey has been, it hasn't been without challenges. Even now, I am constantly working on myself. What stands out most as I reflect on my life is how much of it reflects the lessons I absorbed as a child. These early moments, seemingly insignificant at the time, turned out to be critical in shaping the mindset that allowed me to live life on my own terms.

One memory stands out vividly. I was around 9 or 10 years old when a family friend, Mr. John, visited with his son Kenny to cut my father's grass. I watched as Kenny worked, then saw my father hand him some money. Curious, I asked my father, "How much did you pay him?" He told me the amount, and I felt something stir within me. At the time, I didn't fully understand what it was, but the moment stuck with me. A year or two later, I approached my father with a request: "Can I use the lawn mower to cut grass for money?" My father agreed, on one condition—I had to cut our grass first. After that, I was free to use it as I pleased.

Looking back, that moment was more than just a child's curiosity about money. It was the beginning of a lifelong journey toward independence. Witnessing Kenny being paid for his work planted a seed in me, awakening a desire to earn my own money. It wasn't just about having money; it was about ownership, control, and the satisfaction of being self-reliant. That simple interaction became a defining moment, a divine setup that would shape my decisions for years to come.

THE RESISTANCE TO THE NORM

As I got older, this drive for independence became a defining trait. By the time I was 12, I was cutting grass, shoveling snow, and coming up with little hustles that allowed me to earn my own money. I liked the feeling of being in control, and I wasn't afraid to work hard. This mindset stayed with me into my teenage years, shaping my decisions in profound ways.

At 14, I briefly experimented with a "normal" job. I worked at Burger King for three weeks. After receiving a paycheck for $94, I quickly realized that this wasn't for me. By then, I was already cutting hair in the neighborhood, earning far more in a shorter amount of time while maintaining the freedom to do what I wanted. I couldn't see the point of tying myself down to something I didn't enjoy when I could pursue my own path. Something deep inside me resisted the idea of conforming to a 9-to-5 lifestyle.

Even as I entered adulthood, that resistance remained strong. My father, like many parents, would often ask me when I was 18 and 19 years old, "What do you want to do with your life?" By the time I was 18, I already owned my first barbershop. I didn't have a traditional answer to his question because I wasn't interested in the traditional path. I wanted to build my life on my own terms and didn't even realize I was already doing it when he was asking me questions about my future.

THE IMPORTANCE OF EARLY EXPOSURE

I now see that seeing Kenny cut the grass wasn't just a random moment. It was something I was meant to witness—a glimpse of what was possible. That one experience introduced me to the concept of making money independently of a job, and it became a foundation for the decisions I made later. It wasn't just about the grass-cutting itself; it was about the mindset it planted in me. It taught me that I didn't have to follow the path society had laid out. I could carve my own.

This lesson carried over into other areas of my life. By the time I stumbled upon the opportunity to own a barbershop at 18, I wasn't afraid to take the leap. Many people tried to talk me out of it, warning me about the responsibilities and challenges I'd face. But I wasn't intimidated. My early experiences had already shaped a mindset of independence and self-reliance, and I trusted that I could handle it.

THE DANGER OF EXTERNAL INFLUENCE

One of the biggest obstacles many people face is allowing external voices to shape their decisions. Whether it's parents, friends, or societal expectations, these influences can often lead us away from the path we're meant to follow. When we ignore what's in our hearts and pursue what others think is best for us, we risk living a life that doesn't align with our true purpose.

I've seen this happen time and time again. People spend years chasing a career or lifestyle that others have chosen for them, only to look back with regret. They eventually realize that they were exactly where God needed them to be but failed to act because they let external voices drown out their own. Recognizing and protecting your God-given inclinations is crucial. If you don't, you risk pursuing a life that leaves you unfulfilled.

THE 3 PILLARS PERSPECTIVE AT WORK

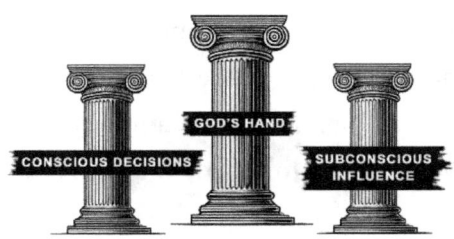

Pillar 1 - God's Divine Hand

God's divine hand was evident in the moment I saw Kenny mowing the lawn—a moment that seemed ordinary but was intentionally orchestrated by Him to plant a seed of independence in my heart. This was not a coincidence. It was God providing a visual example of what was possible: earning money through initiative rather than waiting for someone to hand it to me.

What's more, my father's willingness to let me use the lawn mower—and his condition that I cut our grass first—was also part of God's larger plan, (**Guidance**). These setups remind us that God's interventions often come disguised as everyday occurrences. Whether it's a small gesture, a passing example, or an unexpected opportunity, (**Timing**), His hand is always moving to align us with His purpose, (**Provision**).

Looking back, I see that this moment with Kenny wasn't about grass—it was about God sparking a desire for independence that would guide my path for years to come.

Pillar 2 - Conscious Decisions

While God plants the seeds, it's our conscious decisions that help them grow. Asking my father for the lawn mower, pursuing hustles like cutting grass and shoveling snow, and eventually stepping into entrepreneurship were all deliberate choices that aligned with the independence God was fostering in me.

Each decision became a stepping stone, (**Intentionality**), reinforcing my belief that I didn't need to follow society's traditional path to succeed. At 18, when I took the bold step of owning a barbershop, it wasn't just a business decision—it was a declaration of trust in the values of self-reliance, (**Responsibility**) and creativity that God had instilled in me.

The intentionality, (**Discipline**), of these choices highlights the importance of being proactive, (**Risk**), and bold in pursuing what feels aligned with your purpose, (**Accountability**). Every conscious step you take, no matter how small, is part of the larger journey God is directing.

Pillar 3 - Subconscious Influences

Beyond my conscious decisions, there were subconscious influences at play, rooted in the environment I grew up in and the values modeled by my family. My father's hard work, (**Habits**), and his encouragement to think about my future were subtle yet powerful drivers shaping my internal compass.

He kept asking, "What do you want to do with your life?" because he saw me as both a barber and a barbershop owner but didn't yet recognize that I was already living out my purpose in a nontraditional way. At the time, I didn't fully realize it either.

When I answered, "I don't know," it wasn't because I lacked ambition, (**Motivations**), but because I didn't yet see my entrepreneurial journey, (**Beliefs**), as a valid or "acceptable" standard by society's measures. Subconsciously, however, I was already building a foundation, (**Expectations**), for independence, earning $1,200 a week at 18-19 years old, and creating a life outside the constraints of a conventional job.

INSIGHTFUL WISDOM

1. **Early Experiences Matter**
   The things you see and experience in your formative years often shape your mindset and decisions later in life.

2. **Trust Your Inner Calling**
   The voice inside you that aligns with God's purpose is more valuable than external opinions. Follow it.

3. **Opportunities Are Stepping Stones**
   Small opportunities can lead to great outcomes when approached with faith and intention.

4. **Independence Is a Gift**
   The drive for independence, when aligned with God's will, can be a powerful tool for fulfilling your purpose.

A MOMENT TO REFLECT

Take time to ponder your own life. Ask yourself:

- What early experiences shaped your mindset about work or independence?
- Have you ever felt led to a path but ignored it because of external influences?
- How can you better align your decisions with the purpose God has for your life?

CHAPTER CONCLUSION

Every moment in my story, from watching Kenny mow the lawn to owning my first barbershop, was a divine setup. These weren't random occurrences but intentional moves by a God who was preparing me for a purpose. The same is true for you. Your story, too, is full of moments that are leading you toward the life God has designed for you. Trust in His plan, embrace the lessons, and know that your life is not a coincidence.

TAKE ACTION NOW!

1. PRAY FOR GUIDANCE IN RECOGNIZING OPPORTUNITIES

Why: Seeking God's guidance helps you see divine setups in ordinary moments.

Result: Clarity to recognize and act on God-orchestrated opportunities.

Scripture Reference: "Trust in the Lord with all your heart and lean not on your own understanding; in all your ways submit to Him, and He will make your paths straight." (Proverbs 3:5-6)

2. REFLECT ON YOUR EARLY LESSONS

Why: Revisiting foundational experiences helps uncover the mindset and skills God has been cultivating in you.

Result: A deeper understanding of how God has shaped your approach to life.

Scripture Reference: "Remember the days of old; consider the generations long past. Ask your father and he will tell you, your elders, and they will explain to you." (Deuteronomy 32:7)

3. TAKE INTENTIONAL STEPS TOWARD INDEPENDENCE

Why: Small actions build momentum toward larger opportunities.

Result: Progress in aligning your independence with God's purpose.

Scripture Reference: "Commit to the Lord whatever you do, and He will establish your plans." (Proverbs 16:3)

4. ALIGN YOUR DECISIONS WITH GOD'S PURPOSE

Why: Decisions made in alignment with God's will lead to purpose-filled outcomes.

Result: Greater peace, direction, and confidence in the choices you make.

Scripture Reference: "For I know the plans I have for you," declares the Lord, "plans to prosper you and not to harm you, plans to give you hope and a future." (Jeremiah 29:11)

5. RESIST EXTERNAL PRESSURE

Why: Following God's path ensures you don't compromise your purpose for societal expectations.

Result: Greater focus and alignment with the unique plan God has for your life.

Scripture Reference: "Am I now trying to win the approval of human beings, or of God? Or am I trying to please people? If I were still trying to please people, I would not be a servant of Christ." (Galatians 1:10)

6. EMBRACE SMALL BEGINNINGS

Why: Humble beginnings often lead to significant outcomes when you trust God's timing.

Result: A foundation for future growth and success.

Scripture Reference: "Do not despise these small beginnings, for the Lord rejoices to see the work begin." (Zechariah 4:10)

7. EVALUATE YOUR SUBCONSCIOUS PATTERNS

Why: Identifying habits shaped by your environment helps align them with God's purpose.

Result: Greater self-awareness and a stronger foundation for personal growth.

Scripture Reference: "Search me, God, and know my heart; test me and know my anxious thoughts. See if there is any offensive way in me, and lead me in the way everlasting." (Psalm 139:23-24)

8. FOCUS ON BUILDING, NOT COMPARING

Why: Staying focused on your unique journey ensures you don't lose sight of God's plan for you.

Result: A life built on purpose, not comparison.

Scripture Reference: "Each one should test their own actions. Then they can take pride in themselves alone, without comparing themselves to someone else." (Galatians 6:4)

9. RECOGNIZE GOD'S HAND IN YOUR EFFORTS

Why: Acknowledging God's role in your actions reinforces faith in His divine plan.

Result: Renewed confidence in the steps you are taking toward your purpose.

Scripture Reference: "Now to Him who is able to do immeasurably more than all we ask or imagine, according to His power that is at work within us." (Ephesians 3:20)

10. REVISIT YOUR GOALS AND COMMITMENTS

Why: Reviewing and recommitting to your goals helps align your actions with God's timing.

Result: Perseverance leads to divine rewards.

Scripture Reference: "Let us not become weary in doing good, for at the proper time we will reap a harvest if we do not give up." (Galatians 6:9)

Chapter 5
Divine Connections: Mentors Who Shape the Journey

Life is filled with moments that seem random at first but later reveal themselves as pivotal connections orchestrated by God. For me, these connections came in the form of mentors who imparted wisdom, shaped my mindset, and prepared me for a purpose I hadn't yet fully grasped. These relationships weren't coincidences—they were divine interventions that guided me toward fulfilling God's plan for my life.

DIVINE APPOINTMENTS WITH DAVID AND TYLER G. HICKS

My Story #5: When I was 18 years old, I owned my first barbershop, and it was then that I met David, my landlord. From our very first conversations, David became a mentor who introduced me to principles of business and wealth creation that forever shaped my understanding of success. David was a South Korean immigrant who owned the building where my shop was located, along with several other properties. While I worked every day to build my business, David explained to me the power of leverage—how systems, not just individual effort, could create wealth. He shared that he visited the building only once a month to collect rent from 13 tenants, letting his investments work for him.

This concept of leverage opened my eyes to a new way of thinking. It planted a seed in me to not only work hard but also to work smart. I began to see how I could build systems that would allow me to create passive income, a lesson that would play a major role in my future endeavors. David's influence wasn't just about real estate or business; it was about opening my mind to possibilities beyond what I had seen growing up. God's hand was clearly at work in placing David in my life at such a formative time.

Years later, in my mid-20s, I experienced another divine connection when I met Tyler G. Hicks. Tyler was an accomplished author with over 133 published books on business and real estate. His practical, step-by-step teaching style resonated deeply with me, and I absorbed his lessons in ways I couldn't from anyone else. Reading one of Tyler's books I discovered a phone number towards the end of the book. To my surprise, Tyler answered the phone the very first time I called and invited me to his home in Rockville Centre, one of the wealthiest areas in Long Island, New York.

Meeting Tyler in person was a turning point in my life. Not only did he mentor me in business and real estate, but he also unknowingly inspired me to become a published author myself. His ability to break down complex concepts into actionable steps became a model for how I would later teach and write. Today, as the author of several published books, I can trace much of my approach to Tyler's influence. God's orchestration in connecting me with a mentor who mirrored my aspirations was undeniable.

THE POWER OF MENTORSHIP AND DIVINE TIMING

Both David and Tyler were placed in my life at specific times when I needed their guidance the most. David's lessons came at the start of my entrepreneurial journey, while Tyler's mentorship provided the tools and perspective I needed to scale my ambitions. Each of these relationships taught me something unique, and each was a clear example of God's hand guiding me toward my purpose.

THE 3 PILLAR PERSPECTIVE AT WORK

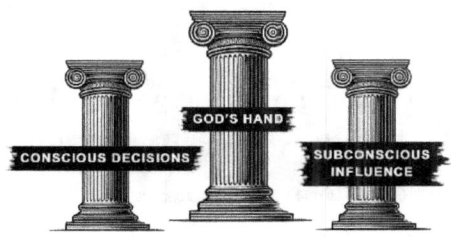

Pillar 1 - God's Divine Hand

God's hand is undeniably evident in the divine setups that shaped this chapter's narrative. Meeting mentors like David and Tyler G. Hicks wasn't just a matter of good fortune or timing; it was a deliberate act of God placing the right people in my path to prepare me for greater purposes. The connections were too precise and the lessons too impactful to be dismissed as random events. David introduced me to the concept of leverage and financial independence at a young age, while Tyler G. Hicks became a mentor who expanded my understanding of business and real estate through his practical and accessible teaching style.

Even the way I connected with Tyler—calling him after reading one of his books and being invited to his home on the same day—was a testament to God's orchestration, (**Favor**). As I reflect on this, I see how God aligned my desire to grow as an author and entrepreneur with Tyler's expertise, (**Divinity**), paving the way for me to become a published author myself. These weren't random encounters; they were moments God arranged to equip me for my journey, (**Guidance**). Similarly, in your life, divine setups often appear as opportunities or relationships that seem ordinary but carry profound significance when viewed through the lens of God's plan.

Pillar 2 - Conscious Decisions

While God's hand is always moving, our conscious decisions play a crucial role in aligning with His plan. The decision to call Tyler G. Hicks after reading his book was a deliberate act of faith, (**Intentionality**). I could have simply admired his writing from a distance, but instead, I took the bold step to reach out, (**Risk**), opening the door to a mentorship that profoundly shaped my understanding of success, (**Focus**). Similarly, the choice to engage with David and learn from his expertise about leverage wasn't coincidental—it was an intentional effort to seek wisdom and apply it, (**Discipline**).

The principle at work here is that conscious decisions are seeds, (**Preparation**). When you make decisions based on faith and alignment with God's principles, those seeds will eventually bear fruit, (**Timing**). However, we often cannot predict the timing of the harvest, as that is in God's control. What may seem like a delayed result is actually God working behind the scenes to bring about the right outcome in due season, (**Accountability**).

Pillar 3 - Subconscious Influences

Subconscious influences are the patterns, habits, and beliefs that shape our actions and results, often without us realizing it. Growing up in a household that valued hard work and determination, I absorbed these traits subconsciously, (**Beliefs**). My father's example of consistency and resilience became ingrained in me, (**Habits**), influencing my drive to seek out mentors and opportunities, (**Motivations**). Similarly, the diverse environment of Queens shaped my openness to learning from people of different backgrounds, (**Adaptability**), a quality that was essential in forming relationships with mentors like David and Tyler G. Hicks.

This pillar also highlights how subconscious patterns can work against us when they remain unexamined. For instance, someone who constantly faces financial struggles might not recognize that their subconscious beliefs about money or their ingrained assumptions are contributing to their challenges, (**Expectations**). The results they experience—whether positive or negative—are not coincidental but are tied to these deep-seated patterns. In my case, the subconscious influences of valuing wisdom, hard work, and openness enabled me to align with God's divine setups and capitalize on the opportunities He presented, (**Guidance**). Reflecting on your own subconscious influences can reveal the unseen forces that shape your life and allow you to make intentional changes to align with God's purpose.

INSIGHTFUL WISDOM

- **Divine Connections Are Intentional:** The people who enter your life with impactful lessons and guidance are part of God's plan to shape your journey.
- **Take Action on Opportunities:** When God places an opportunity before you, act on it with faith and determination. Your response to His setups matters.
- **Mentors Are Mirrors of Aspiration:** The mentors God places in your life often reflect aspects of your purpose and potential that you might not yet see in yourself.
- **God Uses the Unlikely:** Don't limit God's ability to work through people who may be different from you or outside your expected circle.

A MOMENT TO REFLECT

- Who are the mentors or guides that have shaped your journey?
- What steps have you taken to nurture the opportunities God has placed in your life?
- How can you remain open to divine connections that align with your purpose?

CHAPTER CONCLUSION: IT'S NOT A COINCIDENCE

Looking back, I see how meeting David and Tyler G. Hicks, were pivotal moments in my journey—divine connections that were part of God's intentional plan for my life. From David's lessons on leverage to Tyler's influence as a teacher and author, these mentors shaped my path and equipped me with tools I continue to use today.

The same is true for you. God places mentors and opportunities in your life for a reason. Recognize these connections as divine setups, embrace the lessons they bring, and take steps to align with His purpose for you. Remember, it's not a coincidence—it's God's hand at work.

TAKE ACTION NOW!

A clear path to cultivating meaningful relationships and divine mentorships.

1. PRAY FOR DIVINE CONNECTIONS

Why: Asking God for the right mentors and connections helps align your relationships with His divine purpose. For example, just as God brought David and Tyler into my life, He can bring the right people into yours. I prayed for clarity and guidance, and God orchestrated relationships that profoundly shaped my journey.

Result: God orchestrates connections that profoundly shape your journey.

Scripture Reference: "As iron sharpens iron, so one person sharpens another." (Proverbs 27:17)

2. TAKE BOLD ACTION TO REACH OUT

Why: Taking intentional steps to connect with people you admire creates opportunities for growth. For example, I reached out to Tyler G. Hicks after reading his book, which opened doors to invaluable mentorship. Your intentional actions to connect can lead to life-changing relationships.

Result: Intentional actions create new opportunities for learning and growth.

Scripture Reference: "For we live by faith, not by sight." (2 Corinthians 5:7)

3. LEARN TO SEE THE MENTOR IN UNEXPECTED PLACES

Why: God often uses unexpected people to teach us profound lessons. For example, David, my landlord, wasn't someone I initially expected to become a mentor. Yet God used him to teach me invaluable lessons about leverage and business. Reflect on the people around you who might already be offering wisdom or insight.

Result: Discover wisdom and guidance in places you may have overlooked.

Scripture Reference: "Do not forget to show hospitality to strangers, for by so doing some people have shown hospitality to angels without knowing it." (Hebrews 13:2)

4. EMBRACE HUMILITY IN LEARNING

Why: Absorbing lessons from those who have walked the path before you requires humility. For example, I modeled much of my teaching style on Tyler G. Hicks because his practical approach resonated deeply with me. Humility allows you to grow and gain wisdom from others' experiences.

Result: Growth through absorbing wisdom from those who have gone before you.

Scripture Reference: "God opposes the proud but shows favor to the humble." (James 4:6)

5. SOW SEEDS OF RELATIONSHIP

Why: Cultivating meaningful connections requires effort and intentionality. For example, the time I spent engaging with David and Tyler wasn't coincidental—it was an investment in relationships that God used to shape my journey. Take steps to nurture the relationships in your life that align with your purpose.

Result: Meaningful connections grow and yield blessings over time.

Scripture Reference: "Do not be deceived: God cannot be mocked. A man reaps what he sows." (Galatians 6:7)

6. ALIGN YOUR ACTIONS WITH YOUR ASPIRATIONS

Why: Aligning your actions with your goals creates consistency and growth. For example, I wanted to learn about real estate and entrepreneurship, so I pursued mentors who excelled in those fields. Your efforts will yield results in God's timing.

Result: Your actions will lead to growth and alignment with God's purpose.

Scripture Reference: "Commit to the Lord whatever you do, and He will establish your plans." (Proverbs 16:3)

7. EXAMINE YOUR SUBCONSCIOUS PATTERNS

Why: Reflecting on how your upbringing and environment shaped your mindset helps identify barriers and opportunities for growth. For example, my father's hard work and the diversity of Queens influenced my openness to mentorship and learning. Examine how your own experiences have shaped your perspective.

Result: Greater self-awareness and alignment with God's purpose.

Scripture Reference: "Search me, God, and know my heart; test me and know my anxious thoughts." (Psalm 139:23-24)

8. BE A MENTOR WHEN THE OPPORTUNITY ARISES

Why: Sharing the lessons you've learned allows you to impact others for God's glory. For example, just as I've passed on lessons I learned from David and Tyler, look for opportunities to mentor others. Mentorship is a way God uses us to impact lives.

Result: Multiplication of blessings through mentorship.

Scripture Reference: "And the things you have heard me say in the presence of many witnesses entrust to reliable people who will also be qualified to teach others." (2 Timothy 2:2)

9. RECOGNIZE THE BIGGER PICTURE IN RELATIONSHIPS

Why: Understanding that divine connections often serve a greater purpose helps you value every relationship. For example, the mentorship I received from David and Tyler enabled me to help others through my own platforms and teachings.

Result: Recognizing and fulfilling the divine purpose behind every relationship.

Scripture Reference: "And we know that in all things God works for the good of those who love him, who have been called according to his purpose." (Romans 8:28)

10. TRUST GOD'S TIMING FOR RELATIONSHIPS

Why: God brings the right people into your life at the right time. For example, David and Tyler came into my life at pivotal moments, each with a specific role in my growth and purpose. Be patient and trust that God is orchestrating your connections.

Result: Confidence and peace in knowing that God's timing is perfect.

Scripture Reference: "There is a time for everything, and a season for every activity under the heavens." (Ecclesiastes 3:1)

By embracing these steps, you position yourself to recognize and cultivate divine connections that will guide you toward your purpose. These moments and relationships are not coincidences—they are part of God's intentional plan for your growth and success.

Chapter 6
Divine Timing in Union

Marriage is one of the most profound relationships in life, and for me, it has been a journey of growth, challenge, and purpose. While I didn't set out looking for a wife at 22, God had a different plan. When I met my wife in 1997, it was a moment that would shift the trajectory of my life. Looking back, I see that it wasn't a coincidence—it was divine timing, orchestrated to fulfill a greater purpose for both of us.

This chapter isn't just about my marriage but about the way God brings people together for His purposes, often using their unique backgrounds, strengths, and even their weaknesses to shape one another for growth and fulfillment.

A LOVE THAT WASN'T PLANNED

My Story #6: At 22, I wasn't thinking about marriage. I had just embarked on my bachelor years, ready to enjoy my independence and business success. I owned thriving businesses and had no intention of settling down anytime soon. I told myself that marriage was something I'd consider in my thirties. But life has a way of surprising us, and God has a way of rearranging our plans.

I remember my mother asked me to drop two young women home that she worked with. My first thought, as a typical young man, was that I'd try to get one of their numbers. But something in me pulled back, and a quiet prayer emerged: "God, if I could just have one woman to build with, that's all I need."

Shortly after, as I was driving back to my business, I saw her. She was crossing the street, and we locked eyes. We smiled at each other, and something inside me shifted. I didn't know her, but I felt something different. That brief encounter led to a whirlwind romance. Within days, I fell in love with her. By day 11, we were engaged.

At the time, my friends thought I was crazy. "Are you sure you want to marry her?" they asked. I had no doubts. Just a week before, I couldn't have imagined myself getting married. But when I met her, everything I thought I knew about love and commitment changed. It wasn't coincidence; it was divine timing.

TWO BACKGROUNDS, ONE PURPOSE

What makes our story remarkable isn't just how quickly we fell in love but how our vastly different backgrounds came together to fulfill a purpose. My wife had a good childhood, but it wasn't without its challenges. At the age of 12, she experienced something deeply traumatic that left lasting scars. She was taken advantage of in a way no child should ever endure. This, along with a strained relationship with her father, shaped her views on men and relationships.

When we met, I didn't fully understand the depth of her past or how it would influence our relationship. Often, when we meet someone, we only see the surface—the person they present to the world. It takes time, sometimes years to uncover the layers of who someone really is and how their life experiences have shaped them, both good and bad. For my wife and me, those layers would reveal themselves over the years, shaping our marriage and forcing us to grow in ways we never expected.

One of the first instances of this happened 3-4 weeks into our relationship. At the time, I was in business with some longtime friends. My wife, even in those early days, had an intuitive sense that something wasn't right. She told me she believed my business partners were stealing from me. At first, I dismissed her concerns. I had known these guys for years—why would they betray me?

But a few months later, after her persistence, I decided to investigate. She was right. My partners had been stealing from me. That moment solidified two things: her role as my protector and confidant and the fact that her past experiences, though painful, had given her a heightened sense of discernment.

Her ability to detect dishonesty wasn't coincidental. It was born from the challenges she faced in her past—challenges that strengthened her intuition and equipped her to be the partner I needed. God used her pain to develop a gift that would not only protect me but also strengthen our union.

CHALLENGES THAT SHAPE US

No marriage is perfect, and ours is no exception. We've had arguments, disagreements, and moments of doubt. There have been times when I've questioned whether I made the right decision. But every time I reflect on who my wife is and the ways she complements me, I realize that God knew exactly what He was doing when He brought us together.

Many of the challenges we face in marriage aren't meant to break us; they're meant to grow us. Often, the very things we argue about are the areas where God is trying to develop us. For example, where my wife might fall short in one area, it challenges me to grow in patience or understanding. Where I lack, she often compensates with her strengths.

Early in our marriage, I started counseling women in relationships through a website I created called KeepYourMan.com. My wife would often joke that she was my "training ground." At first, I didn't like the comment, but she was right. The insights I gained from our relationship—her struggles, her strengths, and her background—equipped me to help others.

God doesn't waste anything. He uses every challenge, every disagreement, and every shortcoming to shape us for His purpose. What I've learned is that marriage isn't just about companionship; it's about refinement. It's a partnership designed to mold us into the people God created us to be.

THE 3 PILLAR PERSPECTIVE AT WORK

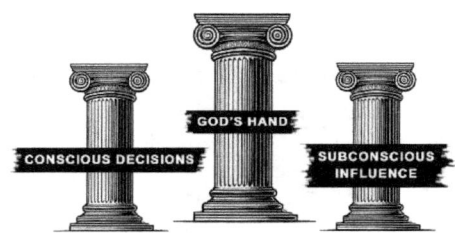

Pillar 1 - God's Divine Hand

God's hand was undeniably at work in bringing my wife and me together. Meeting her at a time when marriage was far from my mind wasn't just a coincidence; it was divine timing, (**Timing**). The seemingly chance encounters—locking eyes as she crossed the street, feeling an inexplicable pull toward her—were all orchestrated by God to fulfill a greater purpose, (**Sovereignty**). That purpose extended beyond just our union; it was about building a family and creating a legacy together.

Over the past 27 years, through highs and lows, this divine setup, (**Divinity**), has remained evident. Four children later, with our youngest just turning 18, the evidence of His orchestration is clear. I often reflect on our journey and think, *There is no way this was a coincidence.* Marriage takes work, and the longevity we've experienced is the result of God's plan unfolding through our lives. His hand has been present in every season, reminding me that even when it was hard, we were part of something greater than ourselves, (**Favor**).

Pillar 2 - Conscious Decisions

While God set the foundation for our union, it was conscious decisions that sustained it. Marriage isn't easy, and ours was no exception. There were times when I didn't fully understand my wife's needs or the challenges she was facing. Yet, I made intentional decisions to remain committed, to forgive when it was difficult, and to love even when emotions didn't make it easy, (**Intentionality**).

These choices weren't always simple, but they were necessary to keep us moving forward. Staying committed, choosing forgiveness, and practicing patience are the seeds that lead to the harvest of a strong and enduring marriage, (**Discipline**). I don't believe the results we've seen are coincidental. A marriage that lasts nearly three decades takes conscious effort, (**Responsibility**).

If you are aspiring to have a successful marriage or any meaningful relationship, understand this: the conscious decisions you make today will determine the outcomes you experience tomorrow. Whether it's choosing to forgive, to listen, or to love selflessly, these acts are powerful and necessary, (**Accountability**). They ensure that the results are not by chance but by design.

Pillar 3 - Subconscious Influences

Subconscious influences have a profound impact on our relationships, often shaping them in ways we don't immediately recognize. For me, growing up in a household where my parents remained committed for nearly forty years provided a model of endurance and perseverance, (**Habits**). Their example silently taught me what it meant to work through challenges and remain dedicated to a union, even during tough times. While I didn't consciously think about this as I entered my own marriage, it's no coincidence that these values became a foundation for how I approached my relationship. This modeling shaped the subconscious patterns that allowed me to prioritize reconciliation and unity, (**Beliefs**).

However, not everyone grows up with positive examples of relationships, and that can influence their own struggles. If you're finding that your relationships are marked by conflict or unmet expectations, it's worth considering what subconscious patterns might be at play, (**Biases**). Sometimes, we unknowingly sabotage our relationships because of what we've absorbed from unhealthy dynamics or a lack of positive role models.

The good news is that these subconscious patterns are not fixed—they can be transformed. Consciously surrounding yourself with people who model healthy and effective relationships can begin to rewire those deep-seated habits, (**Adaptability**). Watching how others navigate disagreements, show affection, or build trust can gradually shift your understanding of what's possible.

Ultimately, the subconscious influences we carry are shaped by what we observe and experience. By choosing to replace unproductive patterns with healthier examples, you set yourself on a path to create the relationships and outcomes you truly want. It's not a coincidence that God places people in your life who can serve as examples—they are tools for growth and transformation.

INSIGHTFUL WISDOM

- **Relationships Are Refinement Tools**: Your partner is often God's way of refining you. Instead of resisting the challenges, embrace them as opportunities for growth.
- **God's Timing Is Perfect**: The people who enter your life—whether romantic or otherwise—often come at exactly the right time to fulfill a specific purpose.
- **Pain Can Produce Purpose**: Just as my wife's past experiences gave her the discernment to protect me, your struggles can equip you with strengths that serve a greater purpose.
- **See Beyond the Surface**: Relationships are deeper than what we initially see. Take the time to understand the layers of your partner's story and how they fit into your shared purpose.

A MOMENT TO REFLECT

Take a moment to reflect on the relationships in your life. Write down your thoughts on these questions:

- How has God used your relationships to shape your growth?
- Are there challenges in your relationship that you can reframe as opportunities for development?
- What strengths does your partner bring that you may have overlooked?

CONCLUSION: IT'S NOT A COINCIDENCE

Looking back, I see how God's timing and design brought my wife and me together. From her ability to discern dishonesty to her strengths that compensate for my weaknesses, everything about our union has been intentional.

The same is true for you. Whether you're in a romantic relationship, a friendship, or a family bond, recognize the divine setups in your life. The people God places in your path are not coincidences—they are tools to shape, refine, and prepare you for your purpose. Embrace the journey, and remember: **It's not a coincidence.**

TAKE ACTION NOW!

A clear path to embrace, nurture, and grow in your relationships.

1. PRAY FOR YOUR RELATIONSHIPS

Why: Ask God to reveal the purpose behind your current relationships and to give you the wisdom to nurture them. When I prayed before meeting my wife, asking for "one woman to build with," God answered in a way that changed my life forever.

Result: Prayer opens your heart to divine insight and helps you see relationships through God's perspective.

Scripture Reference: "I will instruct you and teach you in the way you should go; I will counsel you with my loving eye on you." **(Psalm 32:8)**

2. RECOGNIZE DIVINE TIMING

Why: Reflect on the people currently in your life and consider how their presence might be part of God's plan. Think about the "random" moments that brought you together.

Result: Recognizing divine timing helps you appreciate the purpose and significance of your connections.

Scripture Reference: "There is a time for everything, and a season for every activity under the heavens." (Ecclesiastes 3:1)

3. COMMIT TO INTENTIONAL ACTIONS IN RELATIONSHIPS

Why: Identify one or two conscious steps you can take to strengthen your relationship today. Whether it's a conversation, an act of service, or simply listening better, intentional actions create the foundation for lasting bonds.

Result: Your deliberate efforts will strengthen your relationships and create deeper connections.

Scripture Reference: "Let us not become weary in doing good, for at the proper time we will reap a harvest if we do not give up." (Galatians 6:9)

4. VALUE GROWTH THROUGH CHALLENGES

Why: Reframe struggles in your relationship as opportunities for growth. Challenges refine and deepen bonds when approached with faith and perseverance.

Result: Growth through challenges strengthens your character and builds resilience in your relationships.

Scripture Reference: "Consider it pure joy, my brothers and sisters, whenever you face trials of many kinds, because you know that the testing of your faith produces perseverance." (James 1:2-3)

5. LEARN FROM THE STRENGTHS OF YOUR PARTNER

Why: Reflect on the unique qualities your partner brings to your life. Celebrate how their strengths complement and protect you.

Result: Acknowledging your partner's strengths fosters gratitude and unity.

Scripture Reference: "Two are better than one, because they have a good return for their labor: If either of them falls down, one can help the other up." (Ecclesiastes 4:9-10)

6. MODEL HEALTHY PATTERNS

Why: Consider the examples of relationships you've seen and how they've shaped your understanding of love and commitment. If positive examples are missing, seek out role models to inspire your growth.

Result: Modeling healthy patterns creates a strong foundation for relationships and fosters positive habits for future generations.

Scripture Reference: "Follow my example, as I follow the example of Christ." (1 Corinthians 11:1)

7. CREATE NEW PATTERNS WHERE NEEDED

Why: If past experiences have left negative subconscious patterns, take steps to replace them with healthy habits. Surround yourself with people who model strong relationships and allow their behaviors to influence your own.

Result: Replacing negative patterns with godly habits renews your mindset and strengthens your relationships.

Scripture Reference: "Do not conform to the pattern of this world, but be transformed by the renewing of your mind." (Romans 12:2)

8. TRUST GOD'S HAND IN YOUR UNION

Why: Recognize that your relationship is part of a bigger purpose. Relationships are not just for your benefit but to fulfill a larger plan in alignment with God's design.

Result: Trusting God's sovereignty over your union brings peace and purpose to your relationships.

Scripture Reference: "And we know that in all things God works for the good of those who love him, who have been called according to his purpose." (Romans 8:28)

9. CULTIVATE FORGIVENESS AND PATIENCE

Why: Identify moments where you can practice forgiveness and patience in your relationship. These are not just acts of kindness but seeds that grow into the foundation of a lasting bond.

Result: Forgiveness and patience strengthen the foundation of your relationships and reflect Christ's love.

Scripture Reference: "Be completely humble and gentle; be patient, bearing with one another in love." (Ephesians 4:2)

10. CELEBRATE GOD'S PURPOSE FOR RELATIONSHIPS

Why: Appreciate the ways your relationships shape and refine you. Whether romantic, familial, or platonic, each connection is a divine tool to prepare you for your purpose.

Result: Celebrating God's purpose in your relationships fosters joy, gratitude, and alignment with His will.

Scripture Reference: "Give thanks in all circumstances; for this is God's will for you in Christ Jesus." (1 Thessalonians 5:18)

By focusing on these steps, you position yourself to create meaningful and lasting relationships that reflect God's divine design. These outcomes won't be coincidental—they'll be the intentional results of your faith, effort, and alignment with His purpose.

Chapter 7
No Coincidence When God Calls

There are moments in life when God's call comes so clearly, it redefines everything you thought you knew about yourself and the world. For me, one such moment was when God introduced Himself to me in the midst of profound personal loss and betrayal. It was a divine invitation—one that reshaped my beliefs, deepened my faith, and set me on a completely new path. Looking back, it's clear that everything leading up to that moment—and everything that followed—was not a coincidence. It was God's perfect timing, calling me into a deeper relationship with Him and revealing the purpose He had prepared for me all along.

ISOLATION, BETRAYAL, AND A DIVINE INVITATION

My Story #7: As I reflect on how I met my wife, I realize it was in God's perfect timing for the events that were about to unfold. Betrayed by close friends and business partners, I found myself in a place of disbelief. The people I trusted most were no longer in the picture, and their betrayal left me questioning everything. How did I miss the signs? How could they do this to me? The weight of these questions would often make me think for hours as to what went wrong.

During this time, my fiancée suggested that we attend church together on Easter Sunday. I wasn't against the idea, but I wasn't exactly seeking God either. To me, church was just a place people went to hear good information about God. I didn't have a concept of a personal relationship with Him at that time. I believed in God, but I thought of Him as distant—someone you called on when you needed a favor but otherwise didn't engage with much or have a personal relationship with. That perspective was about to change.

EASTER SUNDAY: THE DAY MY LIFE CHANGED

On that Easter Sunday, the preacher gave a message about Jesus being "the real deal." As I sat there listening, something began to stir inside me. When the preacher gave the altar call and asked who wanted to give their life to Christ, I felt a pull I had never experienced before. I turned to my fiancée and said, "I have to go up there and give my life."

It was as though everything that had happened—the betrayals, the isolation—had led me to that exact moment. Tears streamed down my face as I walked to the altar and surrendered my life to Christ. That day marked the beginning of a journey that would forever change me.

BAPTISM AND THE CALL TO MINISTRY

After giving my life to Christ, I felt a strong desire to learn more about Him. I started attending Sunday school and church regularly, immersing myself in the teachings of the Bible. Three months later, I made the decision to be baptized.

The day after my baptism, I woke up from a vivid dream. In the dream, I was speaking to a large crowd, almost as if I were giving a speech. I told my fiancée about the dream, but we didn't think much of it at the time. Later that day, we went to a Christian bookstore, and as we were about to enter the store, a man named Reverend Johnson approached me. "Young man," he said, "you don't know this yet, but the Holy Spirit just told me that you are a preacher and you don't even know it yet."

I was stunned. His words brought the dream I'd had that morning to the forefront of my mind. Was this a coincidence? I didn't know what to make of it. But over the next several weeks, the same thing kept happening. Random strangers would approach me, asking if I was a minister or a preacher.

Confused and overwhelmed, I called my mother and asked if I could come over to talk. When I told her about the people approaching me, she shared a story that left me speechless. She said, "When you were a little boy, I was walking with you and your siblings down the street. A neighbor stopped me and said, 'Carolyn, your children look so nice today. But that Allen—he's going to be a minister when he grows up.'"

I asked her why she had never told me this before. She said, "I just remembered it now because of what you're telling me."

This revelation, combined with the repeated encounters I was having, confirmed what I had begun to suspect: God was calling me to serve Him.

MIRACULOUS CONFIRMATION

About 13 weeks after my baptism, I attended a church service where the preacher called me out from the back of the room. He asked me to come to the front of the congregation and said, "Young man, people have been coming up to you in the street asking if you're a minister or preacher?"

I nodded, stunned. He continued, "It will keep happening until you accept that God wants you to preach His word."

I looked over at my fiancée, who was in tears. She had witnessed many of these encounters and now saw the confirmation unfolding before her eyes. That moment changed my life, and I accepted God's call to preach his word. From that day forward in 1998, I no longer saw anything in my life as a coincidence. Every event, every encounter, every challenge was part of God's divine order.

I share more details about this journey in my two books *Million Dollar Seed* and *I Will Teach You How to Hear God's Voice.* What I want to emphasize here is how this pivotal moment shaped my understanding of God's purpose for my life and my trust in His plans.

THE 3 PILLAR PERSPECTIVE AT WORK

Pillar 1 - God's Divine Hand

God's hand was unmistakable in every step of my journey during this transformative period. The pain of betrayal, which left me isolated and questioning everything, was not a cruel twist of fate but a divine setup to position me for something greater (**Sovereignty**). God often allows discomfort and loss to redirect us to His purpose (**Intervention**), and my isolation created the perfect environment for me to hear His voice. The timing of my surrender to Christ on Easter Sunday was not accidental; it was God's deliberate invitation to begin a relationship with Him at the precise moment when I had nowhere else to turn (**Timing**).

The repeated encounters with strangers affirming my calling were divine confirmations, orchestrated to remove any doubt about my purpose (**Divinity**). When the preacher called me out during the church service and told me people had been approaching me about ministry, it was another undeniable act of God's sovereign will (**Guidance**). These moments, layered with meaning and purpose, were not random events but evidence of a higher plan unfolding.

God's fingerprints were also present in the revelations from my mother. Her recollection of a neighbor's prophecy about me being a minister as a child further solidified the truth that God's plans are timeless and intentional (**Favor**). What I initially viewed as coincidences—a dream, strangers speaking into my life, a preacher calling me forward—were actually manifestations of God aligning circumstances to reveal His purpose for me (**Provision**). Each of these moments reinforced a fundamental truth: when God has a plan for your life, He will ensure that it comes to pass, even if it means rearranging your circumstances to make it undeniable.

Pillar 2 - Conscious Decisions

While God's hand was moving behind the scenes, my conscious decisions played a vital role in aligning with His plan. Choosing to attend church on Easter Sunday, even though I wasn't actively seeking God, was an intentional step (**Intentionality**) that opened the door for transformation. When I felt the pull to respond to the altar call, it was a deliberate act of surrender (**Discipline**) that marked the beginning of a new journey. These conscious decisions were small but pivotal, setting the stage for everything that followed.

Giving my life to Christ was not just an emotional response; it was a decisive commitment that required me to take ownership of my faith (**Responsibility**). The decision to be baptized three months later was another intentional step. Baptism symbolized my willingness to publicly declare my faith and commit to a life of spiritual growth (**Accountability**).

Sharing my vivid dream with my fiancée and paying attention to the messages from strangers were conscious choices to remain open to God's leading (**Focus**). Investigating these repeated signs, seeking counsel from my mother, and attending church services regularly were all intentional actions that demonstrated my readiness to align with God's will. These moments remind us that while God orchestrates opportunities, it is our responsibility to recognize them and act in faith. My story illustrates that conscious decisions, even when small or uncertain, can have profound impacts when they align with God's purpose.

Pillar 3 - Subconscious Influences

Subconsciously, my past experiences and upbringing had prepared me for this turning point in ways I hadn't realized at the time (**Habits**). My parents' values, particularly my mother's grounding in faith, created a foundation that made me receptive to spiritual truths when the time came (**Beliefs**). Although I wasn't actively seeking God, the principles instilled in me—such as a belief in divine order and the importance of character—shaped my readiness to respond when God began calling me.

My innate resilience, developed through the pain of betrayal and loss, also positioned me to embrace the challenges of this new journey (**Adaptability**). Subconsciously, I was already sowing seeds of faith by remaining open to spiritual possibilities, even when I didn't fully understand their significance (**Motivations**).

The recurring theme of strangers affirming my calling speaks to the power of subconscious influence (**Expectations**). My ability to take these messages seriously, rather than dismiss them as random, reflected an underlying awareness that my life was part of a larger plan. This readiness to discern and interpret spiritual signs was a product of both my upbringing and God's quiet work within me over time.

These subconscious patterns, shaped by years of subtle preparation, allowed me to embrace my calling with confidence when the moment arrived. The subconscious often works in tandem with God's plan, aligning our habits, instincts, and mindset with His greater purpose, even when we aren't fully aware of it.

INSIGHTFUL WISDOM

- **Isolation Precedes Elevation:** Sometimes, God removes people or situations from our lives to prepare us for what's next. Trust the process.
- **Repeated Confirmations** Are Divine Signals: When the same message or theme keeps coming up in your life, pay attention. God often uses repetition to get our attention.
- **Pain Can Be a Catalyst for Growth:** Challenges and losses are not wasted. They are tools God uses to refine us and prepare us for His purpose.
- **Faith Requires Action**: Like Abraham, we must step out in faith, even when we don't have all the answers.

A MOMENT TO REFLECT

Take a moment to reflect on your life. Write down your thoughts on these questions:

- What events or experiences in your life have felt like coincidences but might actually be divine setups?
- How can you shift your perspective to see God's hand in your current circumstances?
- Are there areas where God is asking you to step out in faith?

CHAPTER CONCLUSION: IT'S NOT A COINCIDENCE

Looking back, I can see how every betrayal, every loss, and every moment of isolation was God's way of preparing me for His call and not coincidences at all. Those experiences weren't just random hardships; they were deliberate steps to draw me closer to Him, to confirm my purpose, and to build my faith.

The same is true for you. The challenges you face, the people you lose, and the unexpected turns in your journey are not coincidences. They are moments where God is calling you—inviting you to step into His plan, trust His timing, and embrace His purpose. Listen for His voice, trust in His orchestration, and remember: God's call is never by chance. It's not a coincidence.

TAKE ACTION NOW!

A clear path to recognizing and responding to God's call in your life.

1. PRAY FOR CLARITY IN GOD'S CALLING

Why: Begin by asking God to reveal His purpose for you. When I prayed on that Easter Sunday, even with no intention of seeking Him deeply, God met me where I was and began to unveil His plan for my life.

Result: Prayer invites God to reveal hidden truths and align your heart with His purpose.

Scripture Reference: "Call to me and I will answer you and tell you great and unsearchable things you do not know." (Jeremiah 33:3)

2. PAY ATTENTION TO REPEATED MESSAGES

Why: Reflect on any recurring themes, conversations, or confirmations in your life. Just as strangers repeatedly told me I was called to preach, God often uses repetition to highlight His plans. These are not coincidences—they are divine signals.

Result: Recognizing patterns and messages sharpens your awareness of God's direction in your life.

Scripture Reference: "The Lord will guide you always; he will satisfy your needs in a sun-scorched land and will strengthen your frame." (Isaiah 58:11)

3. TAKE THE FIRST STEP OF FAITH

Why: Even if you don't see the full picture, take a conscious step toward what you sense God is leading you to do. For me, inquiring and seeking further what was happening to me opened the door to a completely new journey.

Result: Taking action, even without clarity, positions you to walk into God's purpose for your life.

Scripture Reference: "By faith Abraham, when called to go to a place he would later receive as his inheritance, obeyed and went, even though he did not know where he was going." (Hebrews 11:8)

4. TRUST GOD'S TIMING

Why: Understand that the isolation or pain you're experiencing might be positioning you for something greater. My betrayal and loneliness created the space for me to hear God clearly and start my journey with Him.

Result: Trusting God's timing brings peace and confidence that He is working all things for your good.

Scripture Reference: "And we know that in all things God works for the good of those who love Him, who have been called according to His purpose." (Romans 8:28)

5. ACTIVELY SEEK WISE COUNSEL

Why: Share your experiences and doubts with people who can provide spiritual insight. When I spoke to my mother, her story about a neighbor's prophecy affirmed God's call on my life. Surround yourself with people who can help you discern God's will.

Result: Wise counsel provides confirmation and clarity as you align with God's calling.

Scripture Reference: "Plans fail for lack of counsel, but with many advisers they succeed." (Proverbs 15:22)

6. EMBRACE THE PROCESS OF REFINEMENT

Why: Be willing to let go of past hurts, betrayals, and failures, knowing that God uses these experiences to mold and prepare you for your purpose. Pain is often the catalyst for growth and transformation.

Result: Embracing refinement shapes your character and prepares you to fulfill God's plan.

Scripture Reference: "Consider it pure joy, my brothers and sisters, whenever you face trials of many kinds, because you know that the testing of your faith produces perseverance." (James 1:2-3)

7. REMAIN OPEN TO GOD'S DIRECTION

Why: Even if His plan seems unconventional or challenges your expectations, stay open. When the preacher called me out during the service, it was a moment I could have ignored, but choosing to listen changed my life forever.

Result: Openness to God's guidance allows you to walk confidently in His purpose.

Scripture Reference: "Trust in the Lord with all your heart and lean not on your own understanding; in all your ways submit to Him, and He will make your paths straight." (Proverbs 3:5-6)

8. LOOK FOR EVIDENCE OF GOD'S HAND

Why: Identify moments in your life where seemingly random events worked together for your good. Just like my dream after baptism, my encounters with Reverend Johnson and others who affirmed my calling, these moments are proof of God's orchestration.

Result: Seeing God's hand in your life reinforces trust in His sovereignty and purpose.

Scripture Reference: "In their hearts humans plan their course, but the Lord establishes their steps." (Proverbs 16:9)

9. PREPARE FOR THE JOURNEY AHEAD

Why: Invest time in learning, growing, and equipping yourself for God's call. For me, baptism and regular church attendance became foundational steps that prepared me for ministry. What steps can you take today to grow in your faith and purpose?

Result: Preparation equips you to handle the challenges and opportunities God has planned for you.

Scripture Reference: "Do your best to present yourself to God as one approved, a worker who does not need to be ashamed and who correctly handles the word of truth." (2 Timothy 2:15)

10. SURRENDER FULLY TO GOD'S PLAN

Why: Acknowledge that your life is not your own and that God's plans are far greater than you can imagine. Commit to following Him, even when the path is unclear or challenging.

Result: Surrendering to God's plan brings peace, fulfillment, and alignment with His purpose.

Scripture Reference: "Then Jesus said to His disciples, 'Whoever wants to be my disciple must deny themselves and take up their cross and follow me.'" (Matthew 16:24)

By taking these intentional steps, you align yourself with God's purpose, opening the door for transformation and growth. The results of these actions are not coincidental—they are the fulfillment of God's divine design for your life.

Chapter 8
The Role of Adversity

Reflecting on my life, I've come to realize that adversity has played a significant role in shaping and propelling me forward. Challenges, hardships, and moments of discomfort have often been the catalysts for growth and transformation, even when they felt insurmountable at the time. While no one enjoys adversity in the moment, I've learned that these trials are often the "gold nuggets" God uses to refine us and prepare us for greater things.

This chapter is about recognizing the divine purpose in adversity. While some experiences are undeniably painful, they are not coincidental. They are part of God's greater plan to bring us closer to Him and to help us achieve the victory He has planned for us.

ADVERSITY AND DIVINE PURPOSE

One of the most difficult concepts for many to grasp is that God allows adversity for a reason. People often question how a loving God could permit suffering, especially when it comes to extreme poverty, violence, or injustice in different parts of the world. They point to these circumstances as proof that God doesn't exist or isn't good.

But to understand adversity, we must first understand the gift of free will. God has given humanity the freedom to choose. His divine instructions, if followed by everyone, would create a harmonious world—a paradise on Earth. However, humanity's free will has often led to sin, selfishness, and destruction. Leaders exploit their people, nations wage war, and individuals make choices that perpetuate cycles of poverty and violence.

God's love for us includes allowing us the freedom to make choices, even when those choices lead to suffering. Adversity is often the result of human actions, not God's design. Yet, in His infinite wisdom, God uses even the worst situations to accomplish His divine purposes.

Romans 8:28 reminds us: "And we know that in all things God works for the good of those who love Him, who have been called according to His purpose." This verse highlights the transformative power of adversity. When we align ourselves with God's will, even the most challenging situations can lead to blessings and growth.

THE POWER OF PERSPECTIVE

The key to thriving through adversity lies in perspective. People may face the same problems, but their mindset determines the outcome. Optimism and faith can turn a crisis into an opportunity.

Adversity is like fire—it can destroy, or it can refine. Those who trust in God's purpose and remain open to His guidance will emerge stronger, wiser, and more prepared for the next stage of their journey.

As I share in the next chapters, many of the difficult situations I've faced—betrayals, failures, and hardships—turned out to be stepping stones to something greater. While they were painful in the moment, they were also necessary for my growth and for fulfilling God's plan for my life.

JESUS: THE ULTIMATE EXAMPLE OF TRIUMPH THROUGH ADVERSITY

Jesus Story #8: To understand how adversity can lead to victory, we need look no further than the life of Jesus Christ. His journey demonstrates how discomfort, pain, and even death can result in the ultimate triumph.

When Adam and Eve disobeyed God in the Garden of Eden, their sin introduced separation between humanity and God. This spiritual separation disrupted the relationship humanity was meant to have with its Creator. Jesus came to reconcile that relationship, but the process required Him to endure unimaginable suffering.

Before His crucifixion, Jesus prayed in the Garden of Gethsemane. In Matthew 26:39, He said: "My Father, if it is possible, may this cup be taken from me. Yet not as I will, but as You will." This moment is pivotal. Jesus was fully aware of the physical agony He was about to endure, yet He surrendered His will to the Father.

The victory of Jesus' resurrection began with His willingness to die to self. By submitting to God's will, He paved the way for humanity's redemption. His suffering was not in vain—it was the price of our reconciliation with God.

Jesus' story teaches us that true victory often requires sacrifice and submission. It's not about avoiding pain but about trusting God's plan, even when it leads through the valley of adversity.

REFRAMING ADVERSITY

Adversity is not just a series of unfortunate events; it's a divine tool for refinement. It forces us to confront our weaknesses, grow in faith, and rely on God in ways we wouldn't otherwise.

In 2 Corinthians 4:17, Paul writes: "For our light and momentary troubles are achieving for us an eternal glory that far outweighs them all." This verse reminds us that our struggles, no matter how difficult, are temporary and purposeful.

Even death, often seen as the ultimate tragedy, is reframed in Scripture as a transition to something greater. Psalm 116:15 says: "Precious in the sight of the Lord is the death of His faithful servants." And 2 Corinthians 5:8 reassures us: "We are confident, I say, and would prefer to be away from the body and at home with the Lord." These verses highlight the eternal perspective God calls us to embrace.

When we trust in God's sovereignty, we can see adversity as part of His greater plan. Instead of asking, "Why is this happening to me?" we can ask, "What is God teaching me through this?"

THE 3 PILLAR PERSPECTIVE AT WORK

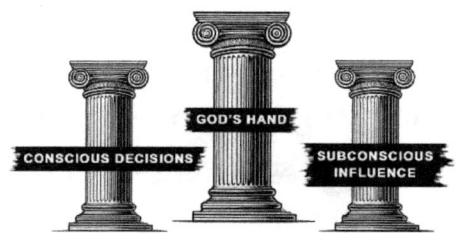

Pillar 1 - God's Divine Hand

Adversity is one of God's greatest tools for shaping us. Challenges that feel overwhelming often serve as divine setups for something greater, (**Intervention**). In my life, moments of betrayal or financial instability were painful at the time but turned out to be pivotal. Through God's hand, these hardships became opportunities to build resilience, faith, and reliance on Him, (**Provision**).

Consider Joseph, who was sold into slavery by his brothers. What seemed like the ultimate betrayal led to him saving Egypt and his family from famine, (**Timing**). Similarly, our own adversities, though painful, are often God's way of aligning us with His greater purpose, (**Sovereignty**).

Every struggle I've faced, from betrayal by close friends to financial crises, was not random but intricately used by God to guide me toward lessons I needed to learn, (**Guidance**). These moments weren't coincidences but clear examples of God's hand refining my life for the future.

Pillar 2 - Conscious Decisions

In times of adversity, our choices matter. Deliberate actions, such as choosing faith, seeking counsel, or aligning decisions with biblical principles, create outcomes that are far from coincidental, (**Intentionality**). During a season of struggle, I consciously prioritized prayer and sought out guidance. These decisions didn't solve everything immediately but created space for God's solutions to manifest, (**Focus**).

When we consciously sow seeds of trust, faith, and hard work during adversity, we align with God's promises. These seeds yield a harvest of breakthroughs, peace, and progress in due time, (**Discipline**).

An example from my life is how, during a business setback, I chose to lean into faith rather than fear. Instead of succumbing to panic, I deliberately sought God's guidance, evaluated my decisions with prayer, and took intentional steps to rebuild, (**Accountability**). Though the recovery was slow, the fruits of those actions were undeniable.

Conscious decisions to trust God, forgive others, and persevere in difficult times are not coincidental in their outcomes. They lead to growth, restoration, and victory aligned with God's plan, (**Responsibility**).

Pillar 3 - Subconscious Influences

Our subconscious, shaped by past experiences and environments, guides our responses to adversity, (**Habits**). For me, the resilience I witnessed in my parents taught me, even subconsciously, to persevere, (**Beliefs**). Without realizing it, these ingrained lessons shaped how I navigated difficulties, (**Motivations**).

If someone's subconscious is filled with negative patterns—such as poor conflict resolution or avoidance—these will impact their outcomes, (**Biases**). However, through exposure to positive role models and environments, the subconscious can be retrained to align with God's principles, (**Expectations**).

My parents' marriage of nearly 40 years demonstrated resilience in the face of challenges. Observing their commitment, even subconsciously, influenced how I approached adversity in my own relationships and decisions, (**Memories**). Without fully realizing it, their example planted seeds that later bore fruit in how I handled trials.

Subconscious influences often feel like instinct, but they are the cumulative result of lessons, habits, and experiences over time, (**Assumptions**). If you find yourself repeatedly facing challenges, consider whether subconscious patterns may be contributing. Through prayer, reflection, and intentional exposure to godly examples, you can retrain your subconscious to align with God's principles for success.

INSIGHTFUL WISDOM

- **Adversity Is a Refining Tool**: Challenges reveal weaknesses and prepare us for greater responsibilities.
- **God Works Through Challenges**: Every hardship has a purpose, even if it's unclear at the time.
- **Perspective Changes Everything**: Viewing adversity as an opportunity transforms your experience.
- **Subconscious Patterns Shape Outcomes**: Positive influences can reframe your responses to adversity.

A MOMENT TO REFLECT

Take a moment to reflect on the role of adversity in your life. Write down your thoughts on these questions:

- How have past challenges prepared you for where you are today?
- What lessons have you learned through hardship that you wouldn't have learned otherwise?
- How can you shift your mindset to see current struggles as opportunities for growth?

CONCLUSION: IT'S NOT A COINCIDENCE

Adversity is not random. It's not bad luck. It's a deliberate part of God's plan to shape us, refine us, and draw us closer to Him. Jesus' journey to the cross and His ultimate victory through resurrection remind us that discomfort and pain are often the precursors to greatness.

The same is true for you. The challenges you face today are not coincidences—they are divine setups for something greater.

Embrace them, learn from them, and trust that God is working all things together for your good. It's not a coincidence.

TAKE ACTION NOW!

A clear path to embracing adversity as a divine tool for growth and transformation.

1. PRAY FOR PERSPECTIVE

Why: Ask God to help you see your current challenges through His eyes. When I faced betrayal and financial hardship, prayer helped me shift from despair to trust in God's plan.

Result: Gaining a God-centered perspective transforms adversity into a stepping stone for growth and trust.

Scripture Reference: "Open my eyes that I may see wonderful things in your law." (Psalm 119:18)

2. ACKNOWLEDGE GOD'S HAND IN YOUR TRIALS

Why: Reflect on past challenges and identify how God worked through them to bring about growth or blessings. This will help you trust His hand in your current struggles.

Result: Recognizing God's hand in adversity strengthens your faith and confidence in His plan.

Scripture Reference: "Consider it pure joy, my brothers and sisters, whenever you face trials of many kinds." (James 1:2)

3. TAKE A CONSCIOUS STEP TOWARD FAITH

Why: Choose an action that aligns with trusting God—whether it's forgiving someone, seeking wise counsel, or committing your plans to Him. When I faced setbacks, leaning into faith rather than fear became the foundation for breakthrough.

Result: Taking a deliberate action demonstrates your trust in God and opens the door for His intervention.

Scripture Reference: "Trust in the Lord with all your heart and lean not on your own understanding; in all your ways submit to Him, and He will make your paths straight." (Proverbs 3:5-6)

4. REFRAME ADVERSITY AS AN OPPORTUNITY

Why: Write down one challenge you're currently facing and list ways it could refine your character or faith. When I began to see betrayal as God's way of redirecting me, it transformed my perspective and renewed my hope.

Result: A renewed outlook on adversity fosters hope and reveals the purpose behind trials.

Scripture Reference: "You intended to harm me, but God intended it for good to accomplish what is now being done, the saving of many lives." (Genesis 50:20)

5. SOW SEEDS OF TRUST AND PERSEVERANCE

Why: Use adversity as an opportunity to plant seeds of prayer, faith, and effort. These seeds will yield fruit in due time.

Result: Faithful perseverance results in blessings and growth in God's timing.

Scripture Reference: "Let us not become weary in doing good, for at the proper time we will reap a harvest if we do not give up." (Galatians 6:9)

6. IDENTIFY NEGATIVE SUBCONSCIOUS PATTERNS

Why: Reflect on whether past experiences have shaped negative habits or beliefs that hinder your ability to thrive in adversity. Replace these patterns with godly principles.

Result: Replacing limiting beliefs with godly truths empowers you to respond to challenges effectively.

Scripture Reference: "Do not conform to the pattern of this world, but be transformed by the renewing of your mind." (Romans 12:2)

7. SEEK GODLY ROLE MODELS

Why: Surround yourself with people who have overcome adversity through faith. My parents' resilience during challenges subconsciously influenced my ability to persevere. Watching others navigate trials with grace will inspire you to do the same.

Result: Learning from role models provides practical wisdom and encouragement for overcoming your own challenges.

Scripture Reference: "Follow my example, as I follow the example of Christ." (1 Corinthians 11:1)

8. TRUST IN THE REFINING PROCESS

Why: Recognize that God uses challenges to prepare you for greater responsibilities. Just as adversity refined Joseph for leadership, God is shaping you for His purpose.

Result: Trusting the refining process deepens your faith and equips you for future opportunities.

Scripture Reference: "For our light and momentary troubles are achieving for us an eternal glory that far outweighs them all." (2 Corinthians 4:17)

9. BE INTENTIONAL IN YOUR RESPONSE

Why: Choose to respond to adversity with faith, patience, and gratitude. These responses open the door for God to work in and through your circumstances.

Result: A deliberate, faith-filled response invites God's transformative power into your life.

Scripture Reference: "Rejoice always, pray continually, give thanks in all circumstances; for this is God's will for you in Christ Jesus." (1 Thessalonians 5:16-18)

10. COMMIT TO GROWTH THROUGH THE PAIN

Why: Embrace the refining process, knowing that God is using this season to strengthen and prepare you for what's next.

Result: Enduring trials with a focus on growth brings spiritual maturity and deeper faith.

Scripture Reference: "Not only so, but we also glory in our sufferings, because we know that suffering produces perseverance; perseverance, character; and character, hope." (Romans 5:3-4)

By taking these intentional steps, you'll begin to see adversity not as an obstacle, but as a tool God uses to refine, strengthen, and prepare you for His greater purpose. The blessings and breakthroughs that follow will not be coincidences—they will be the direct result of your faith, obedience, and alignment with God's divine plan

Chapter 9
Divine Intervention in an Unjust Situation

Life often presents moments that seem frustrating, unfair, or completely random. But as I've come to understand, nothing in life is a coincidence. Even the most unjust situations are woven into God's greater plan to teach us, protect us, or reveal something essential about His divine nature.

This chapter recounts a personal encounter that, while deeply frustrating and unjust at the time, ultimately reinforced my faith in God's ability to intervene and bring truth to light. What initially felt like an unfair attack became a moment of clarity, showing me how God operates behind the scenes, ensuring that nothing—no matter how small—is ever left to chance.

A ROUTINE STOP OR A DIVINE SETUP?

My Story #9: On September 1, 2023, I was preparing to make a deposit at the bank. It was late in the day, just before closing, and I wanted to ensure the funds I had collected from my tenants were deposited before the holiday weekend. As I parked and got out of my car, a police officer stopped me.

He instructed me to get back in my car. I complied, though I was confused about why I was being stopped. When I asked the reason, the officer claimed I had been speeding. When I inquired how fast I was going, he admitted he didn't know. Still, I cooperated and handed him my license, registration, and voluntarily, my firearm permit, as I was carrying legally. I wanted to ensure complete transparency.

The interaction quickly escalated. The officer asked me to step out of my car, and I complied. As I stepped out, he grabbed my firearm. I raised my hands above my head not to be a treat and told him not to pull the gun from my holster recklessly. My voice remained calm yet firm as I said, "I've complied with all your requests, and my firearm is legal. Do not pull it out in an unsafe manner."

I asked for permission to record the interaction. The officer replied, "My body cam is recording," but allowed me to record as well. I retrieved my phone from the car and placed it on the roof to begin recording.

Shortly after, his supervisor arrived. I asked if I had done anything criminal. The officer claimed I had but couldn't articulate what it was. This was both confusing and unsettling. The supervisor insisted they needed to verify my documentation but provided no clarity on the situation. Before I knew it, I was handcuffed.

The stop lasted approximately 15 minutes. During that time, the officer confiscated my phone, wallet, and firearm. At the end of the encounter, the officer issued me a speeding ticket, claiming I had been driving at a high speed—even though he initially admitted he didn't know how fast I was going. My firearm was returned to the trunk of my car, and the incident was over.

THE REVELATION

After the incident, I sat in my car, trying to process what had just happened. Confused and frustrated, I turned to God in prayer: "Lord, what was the purpose of this? What do You want me to learn from this situation?"

Then, I remembered something—I had asked the officer if I could record the encounter after he grabbed my firearm.

When I played back the recording, I was shocked. The officer who confiscated my phone had apparently forgotten it was still recording when he went back to his vehicle. The audio captured two other officers making discriminatory remarks about me. More significantly, a female officer asked the officer who stopped me whether he had clocked my speed. He admitted he hadn't. She then instructed him to return to the location where he had seen me, manually input a speed into the system, and issue the ticket retroactively.

It was clear: the ticket was fabricated.

The week before this encounter, I had been watching videos of people recording interactions with police. Subconsciously, this likely influenced my decision to ask for permission to record during my own encounter. At the time, I didn't understand why I felt compelled to do so, but now I see it was God preparing me for this moment.

The recording didn't stop when the officer took my phone. It continued in his vehicle until my wife's call interrupted it. This wasn't a coincidence; it was divine intervention. The evidence captured on my phone not only provided proof of the fabricated ticket but also exposed the discriminatory attitudes of the officers involved.

THE 3 PILLAR PERSPECTIVE AT WORK

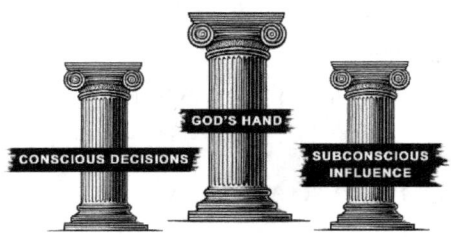

Pillar 1 - God's Divine Hand

God's (**Intervention**) was evident in every step of this encounter. From the unexpected decision to press record during the interaction with the officers to the miraculous preservation of evidence that exposed their actions, His divine hand ensured that the truth would not remain hidden. The recording captured the officers conspiring, revealing their intent to fabricate charges and skip due process, (**Protection**). This was not a mere stroke of luck—it was God aligning events to protect me and preserve justice, (**Sovereignty**).

The way these moments unfolded reflects Psalm 37:6: "He will make your righteousness shine like the dawn, the justice of your cause like the noonday sun." God's sovereignty, (**Timing**), ensured that the lies were uncovered and that I was equipped with the evidence I needed to defend myself, (**Guidance**). This situation reaffirmed that God is always working, even in the darkest moments, to bring about His purposes. When faced with adversity, trust in the unseen ways God orchestrates events for your ultimate good and His glory.

Pillar 2 - Conscious Decisions

The conscious decisions made during this encounter played a pivotal role in exposing the truth, (**Intentionality**). Asking for permission to record the interaction and calmly complying with the officer's initial instructions demonstrated a deliberate effort to act with integrity and caution, (**Discipline**). These actions weren't made with the full awareness of their significance at the time, but they aligned perfectly with God's greater plan.

Choosing to press record, despite the tension of the moment, was a conscious step, (**Accountability**) that safeguarded the truth. Even when I couldn't predict the outcome, taking that small action demonstrated faith and discernment, (**Focus**). It was a reminder that our intentional choices, even in the face of adversity, can create the space for God to work. Reflecting on this, consider how your deliberate decisions—no matter how small—can set the stage for God's plans to unfold.

Pillar 3 - Subconscious Influences

The subconscious influences at play during this incident were equally significant. Just days before this encounter, I had been watching videos of citizens recording their interactions with law enforcement, (**Memories**). Without consciously realizing it, those moments planted the seed of preparedness, (**Beliefs**) that prompted me to press record during this critical situation. It was no coincidence that these ideas were fresh in my mind—it was God preparing me in advance for what was to come.

Additionally, the values instilled in me from an early age, including integrity, resilience, and self-respect, (**Motivations**), shaped how I responded under pressure. My demeanor and actions during the interaction reflected lessons learned over a lifetime,

(**Habits**), even if I wasn't fully aware of them in the moment. These subconscious influences, shaped by God's hand, allowed me to handle the situation with composure and strength.

Our subconscious often carries the imprints of experiences, teachings, and values, (**Expectations**) that God plants along our journey. In this instance, He used those patterns to equip me for a moment of trial. Reflect on your own life: what subconscious habits or lessons might God be using to prepare you for challenges ahead?

YOUR STORY: RECOGNIZING THE DIVINE IN ALL THINGS

It's not always easy to see how God is working in our lives, especially in moments of injustice or hardship. Yet, even in those situations, God's hand is present, ensuring that truth prevails and His plan unfolds.

Think about the events in your own life that seemed unfair or unwarranted at the time. Have you ever experienced a moment where an unexpected turn revealed a deeper truth or protected you from harm? What seemed random or coincidental might have been God's way of exposing what needed to be seen or giving you a defense you didn't realize you needed.

Reflect on these questions:

- Have you experienced a situation where hidden truths came to light in ways you didn't expect?
- How has God provided clarity or a defense in times when you felt powerless?
- What steps can you take to trust God more deeply during moments of uncertainty or perceived injustice?

A MOMENT TO REFLECT

Take a moment to reflect on your own experiences. Write down your thoughts on these questions:

- What moments in your life seemed coincidental but later revealed themselves as part of God's plan to bring truth to light?
- Are there ways God has prepared you, even subconsciously, to handle challenges or injustices?
- How can you respond with faith and trust when you encounter situations that feel unfair or beyond your control?

CONCLUSION: IT'S NOT A COINCIDENCE

This chapter is a powerful reminder that God is present in every detail of our lives, even in the midst of injustice. The police encounter I experienced wasn't random—it was a divine setup to reveal truth, protect me, and remind me of His presence.

The same is true for you. Every challenge, every blessing, and every moment of uncertainty is part of God's plan. Trust that He is working all things together for good. Remember: It's not a coincidence.

TAKE ACTION NOW!

A clear path to trusting God's hand in moments of injustice and adversity.

1. PRAY FOR GUIDANCE IN UNJUST SITUATIONS

Why: Seek clarity and wisdom from God when you face challenges that seem unfair. When I experienced the fabricated ticket, prayer helped me understand God's purpose and trust in His justice.

Result: Prayer strengthens your faith and gives you the clarity to navigate adversity with wisdom and trust.

Scripture Reference: "Commit your way to the Lord; trust in Him and He will do this: He will make your righteous reward shine like the dawn, your vindication like the noonday sun." (Psalm 37:5-6)

2. TAKE CONSCIOUS STEPS TOWARD TRUTH

Why: In moments of conflict or confusion, act with integrity and caution. Just as I chose to record the interaction with the police, align your actions with principles that safeguard the truth and honor God.

Result: Acting with integrity ensures that you are prepared to uncover and uphold the truth in any situation.

Scripture Reference: "The integrity of the upright guides them, but the unfaithful are destroyed by their duplicity." (Proverbs 11:3)

3. TRUST GOD TO EXPOSE HIDDEN TRUTHS

Why: When facing deceit or injustice, remember that God has a way of revealing what's hidden. My recording captured what I couldn't have foreseen, proving that God's timing is perfect.

Result: Trusting in God to reveal the truth provides peace and assurance that justice will prevail.

Scripture Reference: "For there is nothing hidden that will not be disclosed, and nothing concealed that will not be known or brought out into the open." (Luke 8:17)

4. ACT ON SUBTLE NUDGES

Why: Be attentive to subconscious influences or promptings from God. Watching videos about recording police interactions subconsciously prepared me to act decisively during my encounter. These small preparations are often God's way of equipping you for the unexpected.

Result: Acting on God's subtle prompts equips you to handle unforeseen situations with confidence.

Scripture Reference: "Whether you turn to the right or to the left, your ears will hear a voice behind you, saying, 'This is the way; walk in it.'" (Isaiah 30:21)

5. STAY CALM UNDER PRESSURE

Why: When confronted with adversity, maintain composure and faith. Responding calmly, as I did during the police encounter, reflects trust in God and prevents the situation from escalating unnecessarily.

Result: Composure under pressure diffuses tension and reflects God's peace in challenging moments.

Scripture Reference: "A gentle answer turns away wrath, but a harsh word stirs up anger." (Proverbs 15:1)

6. SEEK EVIDENCE AND DOCUMENTATION

Why: In situations where truth may be challenged, take deliberate steps to gather evidence or document events. Doing so can provide clarity and protect you, as it did for me when my recording revealed the fabricated ticket.

Result: Documenting events ensures that truth can be presented clearly, safeguarding against deception.

Scripture Reference: "Everything should be done in a fitting and orderly way." (1 Corinthians 14:40)

7. REFLECT ON PAST CHALLENGES

Why: Look back on moments of injustice in your life and identify how God intervened to bring truth or justice. This exercise strengthens your trust in His sovereignty.

Result: Reflecting on God's faithfulness in the past renews your confidence in His provision for the present.

Scripture Reference: "I remember the days of long ago; I meditate on all your works and consider what your hands have done." (Psalm 143:5)

8. FORGIVE BUT REMAIN VIGILANT

Why: While it's essential to forgive those who wrong you, remain discerning. God calls us to forgive, but He also encourages wisdom in handling relationships and challenges.

Result: Forgiveness fosters healing while discernment ensures protection from repeated harm.

Scripture Reference: "Be kind and compassionate to one another, forgiving each other, just as in Christ God forgave you." (Ephesians 4:32)

9. DECLARE GOD'S JUSTICE IN PRAYER

Why: Speak God's promises over your situation. Declare that He will bring vindication and align circumstances for your good.

Result: Declaring God's justice strengthens your faith and aligns your heart with His will for righteousness.

Scripture Reference: "No weapon formed against you shall prosper, and every tongue which rises against you in judgment You shall condemn." (Isaiah 54:17)

10. TRUST IN GOD'S SOVEREIGNTY

Why: Recognize that even in moments of injustice, God is in control. He orchestrates every detail to bring about His divine plan.

Result: Trusting in God's sovereignty provides peace and assurance that every situation serves a higher purpose.

Scripture Reference: "The Lord will fight for you; you need only to be still." (Exodus 14:14)

By following these steps, you can trust that moments of injustice are not random but are opportunities for God to work powerfully in your life. His hand is always at work, ensuring that no truth remains hidden and no challenge goes without purpose. When the truth comes to light, it won't be a coincidence—it will be evidence of His divine intervention.

Chapter 10
God's Evidence: Exposing the Lies

After reading Chapter 9, you may have sensed that my encounter with the police was only the beginning of a much larger story. What unfolded next brought me into a deeper understanding of God's divine intervention. This chapter reveals how a courtroom battle, a life-altering stroke, and a relentless pursuit of truth became a testament to God's ability to expose lies, bring justice, and transform adversity into triumph.

A COURTROOM BATTLE AND A LIFE-ALTERING STROKE

My Story #10: The fabricated speeding ticket I received led me to consult several attorneys. After reviewing the audio recording from the incident, they confirmed that my Fourth and Fourteenth Amendment rights had been violated. Encouraged by their advice, I decided to file a civil suit against the police department. However, before pursuing legal action, I wanted to address the traffic ticket in court to see if the officer would lie under oath—and he did.

On the day of the hearing, the officer suggested I accept a reduced fine. I declined. Irritated, he maintained his confidence as we entered the courtroom, unaware that I had evidence exposing the truth.

When it was his turn to testify, the officer fabricated an elaborate story. He claimed he had independently determined my speed using proper equipment. I knew this was a lie. As he spoke, I felt my heart racing and my blood pressure rising.

When the judge allowed me to cross-examine the officer, I asked, "Did anyone assist you in determining my speed?" He confidently replied, "No." I followed up, asking about the equipment he used. He lied again.

I turned to the judge and began sharing the truth. I described portions of the recorded conversation, highlighting how the officers had conspired to fabricate the ticket. The judge, clearly surprised, asked, "How do you have this information?"

I explained that I had recorded the interaction with the officer's consent and was prepared to play the audio. But as I prepared to present my evidence, my body began to shut down.

THE STROKE

While speaking, my mouth became unbearably dry, and my words started to slur. I asked the judge for water, but he dismissed my request. When I insisted a second time, someone finally brought me water, but my symptoms persisted.

Struggling to articulate my thoughts, my speech slowed to an almost complete stop. The judge noticed my physical deterioration and called for medical assistance. Paramedics arrived and quickly assessed me, confirming that I was having a stroke.

The courtroom turned chaotic as I was rushed to the hospital. Doctors later explained that the stress of the situation had caused a blood vessel in my brain to rupture. At the stroke unit, neurologists shared the severity of my condition could be life threatening.

Initially, I was filled with anger and frustration. I questioned why God had allowed this to happen. But as I reflected, I began to see a greater purpose. Like Jesus in the Garden of Gethsemane, I needed to surrender to God's will, even amidst immense suffering.

FINDING STRENGTH IN ADVERSITY

Rather than succumb to despair, I chose gratitude, though it wasn't an immediate shift. After being moved to a specialized stroke unit, isolated from my family, I found myself grappling with discouragement and uncertainty. That's when a neurologist came into my room for an evaluation. She shared words that profoundly changed my perspective.

"Mr. Brown," she said, "from the condition you were in, I want you to know that some people are left permanently disabled as a result of the stroke you had. And I also need to tell you, some people don't survive at all." Her words hit me and made me change my perspective about the stroke. Instead of focusing on what I had lost or what could have gone wrong, I began to see the miracle of what had gone right.

God had spared me. What could have been a permanent disability or even death had instead left me with the chance to recover, to reflect, and to live. That moment in the ICU shifted my spirit from discouragement to gratitude. I began to appreciate the small, often overlooked blessings in life—the ability to think, to feel, and to still have time with my loved ones.

When my family visited, the room transformed from one of uncertainty to one of joy and laughter. I made it a point to joke with them, bringing humor into the situation despite the circumstances. I realized that my attitude and faith could either amplify or diminish the hope and encouragement we all needed during this time.

My faith reminded me that God was in control, and I began to view the stroke not as a punishment, but as a tool for growth—a divine reset to reevaluate my priorities. It became clear that adversity wasn't the end; it was an opportunity for transformation.

THE 3 PILLAR PERSPECTIVE AT WORK

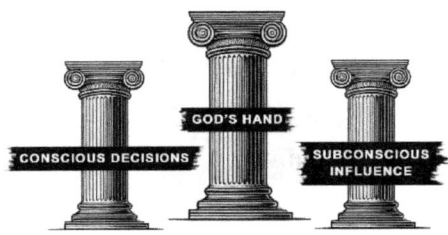

Pillar 1 - God's Divine Hand

God's hand was evident in every step of this situation, from the moment I unknowingly prepared myself by watching videos on recording interactions to the life-altering stroke that occurred in the courtroom. The fact that I had recorded the officers' conversation, which turned out to be crucial evidence of their misconduct, was no accident. Even more remarkable was how the recording device captured key moments despite being confiscated—an act that could only be explained as divine, **(Intervention)**.

God's protection extended beyond the courtroom to my own physical wellbeing. When I experienced the stroke, it could have been the end of my story, but God preserved me. This wasn't a coincidence; it was a reminder that He has a greater purpose for my life, **(Provision)**. Each of these moments was orchestrated to demonstrate His, **(Sovereignty)**, ensuring that truth would prevail and that I would emerge stronger, both physically and spiritually.

Reflecting on these events, I see the undeniable thread of God's divine, **(Timing)** and intervention. What may have seemed like random occurrences were, in fact, intentional steps leading to justice, healing, and a deeper understanding of His power.

Pillar 2 - Conscious Decisions

Throughout this journey, my deliberate decisions played a crucial role in bringing about the truth and achieving justice. Choosing to stand firm in court, despite the overwhelming odds, required faith and courage, **(Discipline)**. Remaining calm during the heated moments of confrontation with the officers and relying on the evidence I had consciously gathered showed the power of intentional, **(Preparation)**.

Filing the civil suit was another bold and conscious decision. It wasn't about seeking revenge, but about holding people accountable and ensuring that the injustices I faced wouldn't be repeated for someone else. Each of these actions reflected a commitment to aligning with God's values of truth and justice, **(Accountability)**.

These decisions remind us that while God works behind the scenes, our conscious decisions must align with His purpose, **(Intentionality)**, perseverance, and faith work hand in hand to bring about results that are far from coincidental. They're a testament to how taking the right steps—even in the face of adversity—can lead to outcomes guided by divine order.

Pillar 3 - Subconscious Influences

The subconscious seeds planted earlier in my life also played a pivotal role in this chapter. The videos I watched prior to the incident, which showcased the importance of recording interactions with police, were not merely entertainment or coincidence. They were, **(Preparation)**. Without even realizing it, those moments influenced my instinct to record the interaction, which became the critical factor in exposing the truth.

Additionally, the values instilled in me by my upbringing shaped how I handled the entire situation. Subconsciously, the lessons of integrity, perseverance, and faith that I absorbed from my parents surfaced in moments of challenge. For instance, staying composed and determined to seek justice was second nature because of those ingrained principles, **(Beliefs)**.

This pillar reminds us that subconscious influences are far from random. They're the culmination of experiences, teachings, and values that God allows to shape our character **(Habits)**. Whether we realize it or not, these elements are tools that align with His plan, often becoming evident only when we look back and connect the dots.

CLOSING THOUGHT

Each pillar demonstrates that nothing in this journey was coincidental. From God's hand ensuring justice, to my conscious decisions in seeking truth, to the subconscious influences that prepared me for the battle, everything aligned to reveal His purpose. These moments show that even in the midst of adversity, God is actively working to guide, protect, and fulfill His promises in our lives.

YOUR STORY: GOD'S EVIDENCE IN YOUR BATTLES

Life's challenges often feel overwhelming, leaving us questioning why they happen. Yet, God is always working behind the scenes, orchestrating events to reveal truth, protect us, and guide us toward His purpose. My story demonstrates how God equips us for every battle, often in ways we don't realize until the moment of need. From preserving crucial evidence to protecting me during a life-threatening stroke, His intervention was anything but coincidental—it was intentional and purposeful.

Now, reflect on your own journey:

- Have you experienced situations where God revealed truth in unexpected ways?
- Can you think of moments when the odds felt overwhelmingly against you, but you later saw how God's hand was guiding the outcome?

God's evidence is everywhere, even in the midst of conflict. He provides us with the tools, courage, and clarity to face our battles. Every challenge you face is an opportunity to trust Him, witness His faithfulness, and prepare for future victories.

INSIGHTFUL WISDOM

- **Trust in God's Evidence:** The evidence you need is often already in your hands. Trust that God equips you with the tools and resources necessary for every challenge.
- **Gratitude Reveals Purpose:** Even in moments of frustration or confusion, gratitude can open your eyes to the ways God is working for your good.
- **Deliberate Steps Yield Divine Results:** Every conscious decision, no matter how small, is a seed that God can use to bring about greater outcomes.
- **God Works Through Preparation:** The habits and subconscious influences you've built over time are often His way of preparing you for unforeseen challenges.

A MOMENT TO REFLECT

Take time to reflect on your own experiences and how they align with God's divine orchestration. Write down your thoughts on these questions:

- What moments in your life seemed insignificant at the time but later proved to be key to overcoming challenges?
- How have you seen God's hand at work in exposing truth or revealing justice in your life?
- What deliberate actions can you take now to align yourself with God's purpose, even in the face of adversity?

CONCLUSION: IT'S NOT A COINCIDENCE

As I reflect on my journey—from the fabricated ticket to the courtroom stroke—it becomes abundantly clear that none of it was random. God's divine plan was evident in every step, ensuring that truth was revealed, justice prevailed, and my faith was strengthened. These events were not mere coincidences; they were intentional setups, designed to draw me closer to Him and remind me of His unwavering presence.

The same holds true for you. Every trial you face, every hardship you endure, is part of God's intricate design. Trust in His plan, take deliberate steps in faith, and remember: **It's not a coincidence.**

TAKE ACTION NOW!

A clear path to exposing lies and trusting God's justice.

1. PRAY FOR GOD'S WISDOM AND STRENGTH TO CONFRONT CHALLENGES

Why: When you're overwhelmed, start by inviting God into your situation. I found strength and clarity through prayer, especially in the courtroom. When you ask God for wisdom, He will guide you through your trials.

Result: Prayer provides strength, clarity, and divine guidance to navigate even the most challenging situations.

Scripture Reference: "If any of you lacks wisdom, you should ask God, who gives generously to all without finding fault, and it will be given to you." (James 1:5)

2. STAND FIRM IN TRUTH, NO MATTER THE COST

Why: When facing injustice, choose to stand firm on the truth. Just as I relied on evidence and integrity to reveal the lies in my situation, you too must trust that truth will prevail when you align your actions with God's principles.

Result: Standing firm in truth strengthens your faith and ensures that God will honor your perseverance.

Scripture Reference: "Let us not become weary in doing good, for at the proper time we will reap a harvest if we do not give up." (Galatians 6:9)

3. TAKE ACTION THAT ALIGNS WITH GOD'S JUSTICE

Why: When pursuing justice, be intentional and bold in your steps. God rewards those who act in alignment with His righteousness. Recording my encounter and presenting evidence in court were deliberate actions that uncovered the truth.

Result: Bold and intentional actions aligned with God's justice ensure that truth and righteousness will prevail.

Scripture Reference: "He has shown you, O mortal, what is good. And what does the Lord require of you? To act justly and to love mercy and to walk humbly with your God." (Micah 6:8)

4. RECOGNIZE ADVERSITY AS REFINEMENT, NOT PUNISHMENT

Why: My stroke seemed like a setback, but it became a moment of transformation. Trust that your struggles are refining you for something greater.

Result: Viewing adversity as refinement allows you to grow stronger and align with God's greater purpose.

Scripture Reference: "And the God of all grace, who called you to his eternal glory in Christ, after you have suffered a little while, will himself restore you and make you strong, firm and steadfast." (1 Peter 5:10)

5. BE GRATEFUL FOR WHAT GOD PROTECTS YOU FROM

Why: After the stroke, I realized how much worse the outcome could have been. Even in hardship, recognize the ways God shields you from greater harm. Gratitude shifts your focus and strengthens your faith.

Result: Gratitude in all circumstances brings peace and deepens your trust in God's protection.

Scripture Reference: "Give thanks in all circumstances; for this is God's will for you in Christ Jesus." (1 Thessalonians 5:18)

6. EXPOSE THE TRUTH, BUT DO IT GOD'S WAY

Why: I could have reacted in anger during the courtroom battle, but I relied on integrity and evidence to let the truth speak for itself. When you face lies or deceit, trust God to vindicate you as you act with honesty.

Result: Acting with righteousness ensures that God's justice will shine through, revealing truth and vindication.

Scripture Reference: "He will make your righteous reward shine like the dawn, your vindication like the noonday sun." (Psalm 37:6)

7. ALLOW PREPARATION TO GUIDE YOUR STEPS

Why: Those videos I watched before my encounter planted the idea to record my interaction. Reflect on the ways God has already prepared you for your current battle.

Result: Preparation equips you to face challenges with confidence, ensuring that your steps are guided by God's plan.

Scripture Reference: "Trust in the Lord with all your heart and lean not on your own understanding; in all your ways submit to him, and he will make your paths straight." (Proverbs 3:5-6)

8. TRUST THAT GOD WILL REVEAL LIES IN HIS TIMING

Why: It wasn't a coincidence that my recording exposed the officers' falsehoods. God's timing is perfect, and He ensures the truth will be brought to light.

Result: Trusting God's timing gives you peace and assurance that truth will prevail in His way.

Scripture Reference: "Do not take revenge, my dear friends, but leave room for God's wrath, for it is written: 'It is mine to avenge; I will repay,' says the Lord." (Romans 12:19)

9. LET GRATITUDE BE YOUR WEAPON AGAINST DISCOURAGEMENT

Why: Even when my body was weakened by the stroke, I chose to focus on God's goodness. Gratitude transforms adversity into a platform for praise.

Result: Gratitude shifts your perspective, allowing you to see God's goodness even in difficult times.

Scripture Reference: "Do not be anxious about anything, but in every situation, by prayer and petition, with thanksgiving, present your requests to God. And the peace of God, which transcends all understanding, will guard your hearts and your minds in Christ Jesus." (Philippians 4:6-7)

10. SOW INTEGRITY TO REAP VICTORY

Why: Every conscious decision rooted in integrity—like recording evidence and remaining calm—creates a foundation for God's justice to prevail. Trust that what you sow will produce results in God's timing.

Result: Sowing integrity ensures that you will experience victory aligned with God's will.

Scripture Reference: "The wicked earn deceptive wages, but whoever sows righteousness reaps a sure reward." (Proverbs 11:18)

By following these steps, you align with God's principles and open the door for His justice to prevail. Each decision you make with integrity and faith will lead to outcomes that are far from coincidental—they are the intentional works of a sovereign God. Trust that His plan is unfolding perfectly, and His justice will shine through in your life.

Chapter 11
A Stroke of Purpose: No Coincidence

COMING HOME AFTER THE STROKE

My Story #11: When I returned home from the hospital, life was not the same. The stroke had impacted me physically and emotionally, leaving my speech altered and my right hand immobilized. For someone who relied on their right hand for everything—typing, writing, and handling daily tasks—this was a major adjustment.

I could still communicate, but my voice sounded noticeably different. If you'd heard me speak before and after the stroke, you'd immediately notice the change caused by muscle and nerve damage in my mouth. Even now, I operate at about 85% to 90% capacity. While I'm not fully back to normal, I thank God for the progress I've made.

The biggest hurdle was my right hand. Everything I did required its use, and I couldn't imagine functioning without it. After a week of resting at home, I attempted to return to work. But sitting at my desk, unable to accomplish simple tasks, left me frustrated and discouraged. I would leave my desk, retreat to bed, and wonder when—or if—I'd ever regain full mobility. Yet, as you'll see by the end of this chapter, God used this trial to bring about purpose and blessings far beyond what I could have imagined.

A DIVINE INTRODUCTION TO ARTIFICIAL INTELLIGENCE

Two days before my stroke, on November 12, 2023, I visited my mother in Queens, New York. Around the same time, my friend Greg was visiting his mother, also in Queens. We decided to meet at Greg's mom's house, where we caught up and shared updates on our lives.

During our conversation, Greg introduced me to two artificial intelligence tools: Bard and ChatGPT. While I had heard about AI before, I had never explored it in depth. At first, I didn't see the significance. Greg encouraged me to type something into the AI chat, saying, "Hey AI, type in something you're working on."

Skeptical but curious, I asked the AI about a website project I had launched the year prior. What happened next left me speechless. The AI's response validated ideas I had already considered and even offered new insights that resonated deeply with my vision. It confirmed the uniqueness of what I was building in the market—a concept no one else had explored.

That night, I spent hours experimenting with the tools, inputting prompts, and marveling at the responses. Greg had opened my eyes to the incredible potential of AI, and I immediately downloaded the tools to my phone, eager to explore them further.

DISCOVERING PURPOSE DURING RECOVERY

Two days later, I suffered my stroke. Lying in the hospital, grappling with the physical and emotional toll, I found solace in the AI tools Greg had shown me. When visiting hours ended and my family went home, I would spend hours using ChatGPT and Bard, amazed at how they engaged me intellectually and creatively.

The nurses frequently reminded me to lower my voice, as I was disturbing other patients late into the night. I would apologize, but inside, I was energized. These tools became an outlet for me, helping me stay productive and focused even as I recovered.

When I returned home, however, the limitations of my right hand quickly became apparent. Tasks I had taken for granted—typing emails, creating blog posts, and managing projects—were now daunting. I fell behind on work, drowning in unanswered emails and incomplete assignments.

One day, as I lay in bed feeling defeated, I remembered that there were voice-to-text tools available. I experimented with Google Docs' voice typing tool, and it was a game changer. I began dictating emails, blog posts, and documents, using my left hand to copy and paste. The process was slow at first, but it reignited my productivity. This newfound efficiency planted a bold idea: If I could dictate blog posts, could I also dictate an entire book?

REDISCOVERING THE PROPHECY

By January 2024, I had completed my second book, *Residual Income for Music Producers*, despite the challenges of my recovery. Encouraged by this achievement, I set a bold goal: to write a book every month for the rest of the year.

In February 2024, while working on my third book, my son came into my office. Seeing me focused on another writing project, he asked a question about my first book, *Million Dollar Seed*. Curious, I pulled out the book to find the answer, and as I flipped through the pages, I was stunned by what I saw.

There, in my own words, was the prophecy God had given me back in 2020: "You will release books every month in the future." I had completely forgotten about this declaration. At the time, I had doubted it was possible. Writing *Million Dollar Seed* had taken me over four months, and as someone who types slowly and doesn't consider themselves a writer, the idea of releasing books monthly seemed far-fetched.

What amazed me even further was that in the same chapter of *Million Dollar Seed*, I had documented confirmations from my two friends, Dion and Rockwilder. Dion had said to me, "After seeing your first book, I can see you releasing books every month." At the time, I laughed, doubting it could happen. Rockwilder had also unknowingly echoed the prophecy when I told him I completed my first book, asking me, "How many books have you written?" When I corrected him, saying it was just one, he insisted, "No, I could've sworn you said books."

These confirmations, spoken by two different people, were recorded alongside God's prophecy in my book for years prior, yet I had forgotten about them entirely. Rediscovering these words in 2024 while actively pursuing the goal of writing books every month was a profound moment. I realized I was walking in the very prophecy God had spoken to me four years earlier—a prophecy I had doubted because I couldn't see how it would come to pass.

This rediscovery reminded me of the importance of trusting God's word, even when the path seems unclear. At the time, I judged God's promise based on my own limitations. I didn't see the tools that would later make it possible: the voice-to-text software, artificial intelligence, and the inspiration born from my recovery. But God, in His infinite wisdom, saw it all and prepared the way.

UNEXPECTED HEALTH BLESSINGS

The stroke also brought an unexpected blessing: significant weight loss. For years, I had prayed for the discipline to lose weight, but nothing worked. After the stroke, I temporarily lost my sense of taste—a condition affecting about 30% of stroke survivors.

The only foods I could taste were fruits and vegetables. Everything else tasted bland, like cardboard. I would ask my wife if she was using seasoning because I couldn't taste anything. This restriction, though frustrating at first, became a blessing. With my appetite limited to healthy options, I lost between 50 and 60 pounds, improving my overall health and energy levels.

SEEING THE BIGGER PICTURE

Looking back, it's clear that every part of this journey was orchestrated by God. The stroke wasn't a setback—it was a setup for something greater. The tools I discovered, the weight I lost, and the books I wrote were all part of His divine plan. Even my ongoing civil case against the police is serving a purpose, bringing awareness to issues that need reform.

God's ways are not our ways, but His plans are always for our good.

THE 3 PILLAR PERSPECTIVE AT WORK

Pillar 1 - God's Divine Hand

God's presence in this chapter is evident in every moment and every revelation. The stroke, while appearing to be a devastating event, was actually a tool in God's hands to fulfill His promises and bring me into a deeper understanding of His purpose **(Intervention)**. Before the stroke even happened, God had already set the stage by orchestrating my meeting with Greg. It wasn't by chance that both of us were visiting our mothers in Queens at the same time. That connection wasn't random—it was a divine appointment **(Timing)**. Greg's introduction to AI wasn't just a casual suggestion; it was God equipping me with tools I would need for the season ahead, **(Provision)**.

The timing of the stroke, though difficult, further underscored God's divine orchestration, **(Sovereignty)**. Just two days after being introduced to the AI tools, I found myself grappling with physical limitations that would have otherwise halted my work. But God had already provided the solution, ensuring that I had the means to stay productive, **(Favor)**. Without the stroke, I might never have fully embraced the tools or seen their potential. God's hand not only preserved my life during the stroke but also turned it into an opportunity for growth and fulfillment.

Years before, God had spoken to me about writing books every month, a prophecy that seemed impossible at the time. I doubted, relying on my own limitations rather than trusting His vision. Yet here I was, recovering from the stroke, actively fulfilling that prophecy. This was not coincidence; it was God's faithfulness manifesting through His perfect timing and planning **(Guidance)**. Every element of this chapter—the introduction to AI, the timing of the stroke, and the rediscovery of His promises—bears His unmistakable fingerprints.

Pillar 2 - Conscious Decisions

The decisions I made throughout this chapter were pivotal in shaping its outcome. Choosing to explore the AI tools Greg introduced was not just a casual decision but a deliberate act of curiosity and willingness to learn, **(Intentionality)**. Engaging with these tools laid the groundwork for productivity during a time when my physical limitations could have left me idle. It wasn't clear to me then how important these tools would become, but the conscious decision of embracing them proved transformative.

When I discovered voice-to-text tools, it was another conscious decision to adapt to my circumstances rather than surrender to them **(Adaptability)**. I refused to let the stroke define me or limit my purpose. Instead of focusing on what I couldn't do, I chose to find ways to work around my limitations. This decision led me to new levels of creativity and efficiency, turning adversity into opportunity **(Discipline)**.

Setting the goal to write books monthly was another bold, intentional step **(Responsibility)**. It wasn't something I had to do, especially given my recovery. But I made the choice to challenge myself, trusting that God would provide the strength and inspiration to follow through. Each book became a testament to faith in action, proving that conscious decisions aligned with God's plan can lead to incredible outcomes, **(Accountability)**. These actions were not coincidental; they were deliberate steps guided by faith and perseverance.

Pillar 3 - Subconscious Influences

Subconscious influences also played a significant role in this chapter. My innate curiosity and openness to innovation are qualities God planted in me long ago, **(Motivations)**. Without consciously planning it, these traits prepared me to embrace the AI tools Greg introduced. I didn't hesitate to experiment and explore because seeking out new solutions and resources is second nature to me. This internal drive became essential in overcoming the challenges I faced during recovery, **(Beliefs)**.

The timing of my meeting with Greg and the introduction to AI was another reflection of subconscious alignment with God's plan. While I didn't orchestrate the encounter, my habits of staying connected and maintaining relationships positioned me exactly where I needed to be, **(Habits)**. It wasn't a deliberate decision to meet that day, but it was part of a God-ordained pattern that brought about His purpose.

Even the decision to use voice dictation, initially driven by necessity, reflects a deeper subconscious resilience. Without fully realizing it, I chose to focus on solutions rather than limitations, adapting to circumstances in ways that allowed me to continue pursuing my goals, **(Expectations)**. Subconsciously, I was also responding to God's earlier promises. Though I didn't see how they would come to pass, the belief in their eventual fulfillment motivated me to keep pushing forward.

God often works through the habits, patterns, and instincts He has instilled in us. These subconscious tendencies, when aligned with His purpose, become tools He uses to guide us toward His plans. The events of this chapter demonstrate how God's work is never random; even the instincts and traits He places within us are part of His intentional design to prepare us for what lies ahead.

INSIGHTFUL WISDOM

- **Challenges Are Opportunities:** What feels like a setback may be God's way of refining you or aligning you with His purpose.

- **Prophecies Come with Preparation:** God reveals His promises in advance, knowing the tools and paths you'll need to fulfill them. Trust His foresight and timing.
- **Tools Are Divine Gifts:** The resources and innovations God places in your life are not coincidental—they're strategic for your growth and purpose. Embrace them with faith.
- **Gratitude Shifts Perspective:** Focusing on what you have, even in adversity, reveals the blessings hidden in every challenge.

A MOMENT TO REFLECT

- Can you recall a time when a challenge became the gateway to a blessing or breakthrough?
- What tools, relationships, or resources has God provided that have transformed your journey?
- Are you living out a promise or prophecy that once seemed impossible? If so, how did God prepare you for it?

CONCLUSION: TRUSTING THE DIVINE PLAN

Looking back on my journey, especially after my stroke, it's undeniable that God's hand has been guiding me. What seemed like a moment of loss turned into a setup for innovation, fulfillment, and transformation. Each challenge became an opportunity, and each opportunity aligned perfectly with promises God made years before.

This journey has taught me—and I hope teaches you—that nothing in life is random or coincidental. Every trial, every triumph, and every resource has been part of a divine plan. When we trust God, even the most painful moments can become the foundation for His greatest work in our lives. Faith assures us that every challenge has purpose and that every setback is preparation for the fulfillment of His promises.

Remember: your life is not a coincidence. Trust the process and watch His plan unfold.

TAKE ACTION NOW!

A clear path to turning setbacks into divine opportunities.

1. EMBRACE CHALLENGES AS GOD'S REFINING PROCESS

Why: View your obstacles as a setup for God's purpose rather than a setback. My stroke seemed like a devastating event, but it became the gateway to discovering tools and fulfilling prophecies.

Result: Facing trials with faith will strengthen and refine you, aligning you with God's greater plan.

Scripture Reference: "And the God of all grace, who called you to his eternal glory in Christ, after you have suffered a little while, will himself restore you and make you strong, firm and steadfast." (1 Peter 5:10)

2. TRUST GOD'S TIMING, EVEN WHEN IT SEEMS DELAYED

Why: Prophecies may feel distant or impossible, but God's timing is perfect. Rediscovering the prophecy about writing monthly books during my recovery proved that He always fulfills His promises.

Result: Trusting God's timing will bring His promises to fruition exactly when they're meant to manifest.

Scripture Reference: "For the revelation awaits an appointed time; it speaks of the end and will not prove false. Though it

linger, wait for it; it will certainly come and will not delay."
(Habakkuk 2:3)

3. RECOGNIZE TOOLS AND RESOURCES AS DIVINE GIFTS

Why: The AI tools I discovered before my stroke weren't coincidences—they were God's provision for my recovery. Identify and embrace the tools God places in your path, knowing they're part of His plan.

Result: Acknowledging God's provision equips you with the resources needed to fulfill His purpose for your life.

Scripture Reference: "And God is able to bless you abundantly, so that in all things at all times, having all that you need, you will abound in every good work." (2 Corinthians 9:8)

4. ADAPT TO YOUR CIRCUMSTANCES WITH CREATIVITY

Why: Don't let limitations define your future. I couldn't use my right hand, but discovering voice-to-text solutions allowed me to keep working toward my goals. Find ways to adapt, trusting that God will provide solutions.

Result: Creative adaptation enables you to overcome obstacles and continue working toward God's purpose.

Scripture Reference: "The Lord makes firm the steps of the one who delights in Him; though he may stumble, he will not fall, for the Lord upholds him with His hand." (Psalm 37:23-24)

5. STAY OPEN TO INNOVATION AND CHANGE

Why: God often works through new and unfamiliar methods to guide us. My willingness to explore AI technology positioned me to continue fulfilling my purpose despite my limitations. Be open to trying new things as God leads.

Result: Openness to God's guidance leads to clarity and new opportunities aligned with His purpose.

Scripture Reference: "Trust in the Lord with all your heart and lean not on your own understanding; in all your ways submit to him, and he will make your paths straight." (Proverbs 3:5-6)

6. REVISIT PAST PROMISES AND PROPHECIES

Why: Reflect on words or visions God has spoken into your life. Rediscovering the prophecy about writing books reignited my faith and showed me that God's plans were already in motion.

Result: Remembering God's promises strengthens your faith and motivates you to persevere.

Scripture Reference: "I will remember the deeds of the Lord; yes, I will remember your miracles of long ago. I will consider all your works and meditate on all your mighty deeds." (Psalm 77:11-12)

7. SHIFT YOUR FOCUS TO GRATITUDE

Why: Gratitude for small victories, like my improved health and weight loss, transformed my perspective during recovery. Focus on what you have rather than what you've lost, and you'll see God's blessings more clearly.

Result: Gratitude cultivates peace and strengthens your trust in God's goodness.

Scripture Reference: "Do not be anxious about anything, but in every situation, by prayer and petition, with thanksgiving, present your requests to God. And the peace of God, which transcends all understanding, will guard your hearts and your minds in Christ Jesus." (Philippians 4:6-7)

8. TAKE BOLD STEPS TOWARD YOUR PURPOSE

Why: Setting a goal to write books monthly seemed impossible, but trusting God and taking that first step allowed me to achieve what once felt out of reach. Start small, but start now.

Result: Bold steps of faith lead to progress and open doors aligned with God's purpose.

Scripture Reference: "Commit to the Lord whatever you do, and he will establish your plans." (Proverbs 16:3)

9. VIEW LIMITATIONS AS OPPORTUNITIES FOR INNOVATION

Why: My inability to write forced me to explore voice tools, leading to greater productivity. Consider how your current challenges could inspire new, better ways of achieving your goals.

Result: Viewing limitations as opportunities fosters innovation and growth.

Scripture Reference: "See, I am doing a new thing! Now it springs up; do you not perceive it? I am making a way in the wilderness and streams in the wasteland." (Isaiah 43:19)

10. TRUST THAT NOTHING IS A COINCIDENCE

Why: The meeting with Greg, the AI tools, and even the stroke were all aligned to fulfill God's purpose. Trust that every event, no matter how difficult, is part of a divine setup.

Result: Believing in God's sovereignty brings clarity and peace as you navigate life's challenges.

Scripture Reference: "And we know that in all things God works for the good of those who love him, who have been called according to his purpose." (Romans 8:28)

Each trial, resource, and opportunity you encounter is part of a divine plan orchestrated by God. Challenges like my stroke, introductions to innovative tools, and moments of clarity were not random—they were purposefully aligned to fulfill His promises. Trust that your own journey, with its setbacks and breakthroughs, is leading to outcomes that reflect God's intentional design. When the pieces come together, you'll know: it wasn't coincidence—it was God all along.

Chapter 12
A Journey of Reconnection: From Mentor to Conflict

THE FOUNDATION OF A MENTORSHIP

My Story #12: Life is full of relationships that are divinely orchestrated to teach, shape, and prepare us for the path God has set. Some relationships guide us, others challenge us, and a few do both simultaneously. My connection with David was one of those rare bonds. Starting as my mentor and landlord when I first opened my barbershop at eighteen in 1992, David introduced me to foundational principles of business and resilience. Over the years, David's mentorship planted seeds of wisdom that would take decades to fully understand.

In 1997, David and his wife, Jeannie, sold their New York properties and purchased a 56-acre retreat center in Pennsylvania. They transformed the property into a Christian retreat center, aiming to create a sanctuary for ministry and renewal. Though our interactions became less frequent, I would occasionally visit the retreat center, and our connection remained intact.

A DIVINE RECONNECTION

In 2007, my mother inquired about a place to host a church retreat. I suggested we visit David's retreat center in Pennsylvania, thinking it could be a suitable venue. When we arrived, David wasn't there. Instead, we were greeted by Jeannie. This meeting was no coincidence—it was the beginning of a series of divine setups that would alter my life's course.

Jeannie and I caught up during that visit, and she inquired about my work. When I explained my success in online business, she expressed a desire to partner with me to bring visibility and modernization to the retreat center. Jeannie shared that she had purchased David's share of the property for $1 million and was now the sole owner. This revelation was surprising, as I had assumed David still managed the center. Unbeknownst to me, Jeannie's ownership and the strain it caused between her and David were key pieces of the puzzle God was aligning.

After prayerful consideration and receiving confirmation, my wife and I decided to move to the property in July 2008. While I felt this was a divine opportunity, my wife had reservations. She often expressed that something didn't feel quite right. In hindsight, her discernment was accurate, as we would later uncover many hidden challenges.

THE FORMATION OF A BUSINESS PARTNERSHIP

Initially, Jeannie and I collaborated to create a ministry, but our visions didn't align, and the initiative stalled. About nine months after moving to the property, we shifted our focus to the retreat center's business potential. Together, we formed the Christian Life Retreat Center, with Jeannie holding 51% ownership and me holding 49%.

I took charge of marketing and technology, bringing in church groups and managing the website. Jeannie oversaw operations, including housekeeping and event logistics. Business began to grow, but cracks in our partnership soon appeared. Jeannie frequently mentioned that the property was struggling financially, citing back taxes and unpaid group fees as reasons why I couldn't receive my share of the profits. I trusted her judgment and even allowed her to use $40,000 from a large booking to cover taxes. However, as time passed, her excuses became harder to believe.

THE DISCOVERY OF HIDDEN FUNDS

Despite our growing bookings, I wasn't receiving my agreed-upon 49% share of the revenue. Jeannie often claimed that groups hadn't paid or that she was donating their stays to churches in need. This didn't sit right with me. I began tracking the groups and suspected significant discrepancies between her reports and the actual earnings.

The breakthrough came one Sunday after church. My wife, with her sharp intuition, asked, "What about the PNC account you and Jeannie opened a year and a half ago?" Acting on her hunch, I checked the account. To my shock, I discovered over $230,000 in deposits—funds Jeannie had hidden. Matching canceled checks from church groups to deposit dates confirmed that this money came from the retreat business.

This revelation led to a heated confrontation with Jeannie. She admitted to the financial secrecy but tried to downplay its significance. The discovery also strained my relationship with David, who had been unaware of my business dealings with Jeannie. Despite no longer owning the property, David had lingering financial disputes with Jeannie, and she had explicitly asked me not to involve him. This secrecy only added to the tension.

THE COURT BATTLE AND JEANNIE'S PASSING

Unable to resolve the conflict privately, I filed a legal claim against Jeannie in 2011. The evidence we gathered—including her admissions during depositions—strengthened my case. Tragically, Jeannie passed away in 2013 before the case was resolved.

However, her testimony, recorded before her death, was instrumental in securing a judgment in my favor in 2016.

After Jeannie's passing, David became the estate administrator, and our interactions during court proceedings were strained. He refused to speak to me during appearances, and the animosity between us grew deeper. Despite the challenges, I began to see how God was using these trials to refine me. The retreat center was more than a business—it was a crucible for growth, teaching me lessons in patience, discernment, and unwavering faith.

MISSED OPPORTUNITIES AND GOD'S TIMING

Before our partnership officially began, Jeannie had offered to transfer the property deed into my name. She instructed me to go to the county clerk's office to complete the paperwork, but I delayed. Within 30 days, our partnership soured, and the opportunity slipped away. Reflecting on this missed chance, I see God's hand at work. Perhaps the timing wasn't right, or there were lessons I still needed to learn.

PREPARING FOR RECONNECTION

After the court case concluded in 2016, I had no contact with David for nearly eight years. Our relationship seemed irreparably broken. Then, in January 2024, a surprising event brought us back into each other's lives. This reconnection, sparked by a lie from David's adopted son, marked the beginning of a new chapter—one that will be explored in the next part of this story.

THE 3 PILLAR PERSPECTIVE AT WORK

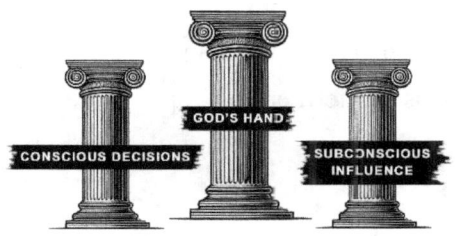

Pillar 1 - God's Divine Hand

Throughout this chapter, God's hand was evident in orchestrating every step of the journey. The meeting with Jeannie in 2007, instead of David, was a pivotal moment that led to opportunities I didn't foresee at the time, **(Timing)**. It wasn't a random occurrence—it was God setting the stage for what was to come, **(Sovereignty)**. Jeannie's ownership of the property, her willingness to partner with me, and even her eventual offer to transfer the property deed were all markers of God's intricate planning, **(Guidance)**.

While I didn't finalize the deed transfer, this wasn't a misstep. It was a reflection of God's timing, ensuring that the larger purpose He had for the property would unfold when the time was right **(Intervention)**. Jeannie's offer symbolized a spiritual transfer, a declaration of what was meant to be, even if the full realization would come later. The entire process was a reminder that God's plans often span beyond our immediate understanding and that His timing is always perfect, even when it seems delayed from our perspective, **(Provision)**.

Pillar 2 - Conscious Decisions

Conscious decisions played a critical role in navigating the complexities of this journey. From agreeing to move my family to

Pennsylvania to forming the partnership with Jeannie, these choices were rooted in faith and a desire to align with God's purpose, **(Intentionality)**. Partnering with Jeannie to create the Christian Life Retreat Center was a deliberate step to make the most of the opportunities presented, even though challenges arose later, **(Accountability)**.

When discrepancies in finances surfaced, my decision to confront the situation, track the group payments, and eventually file a legal claim against Jeannie was a reflection of my commitment to integrity and justice, **(Responsibility)**. These actions weren't easy, but they aligned with God's principles of accountability and stewardship, **(Discipline)**. Choosing to stay firm in my faith and pursue the truth, despite the strain on relationships, demonstrated a conscious alignment with God's greater purpose, **(Risk)**.

Pillar 3 - Subconscious Influences

Subconsciously, years of mentorship under David and the lessons I had learned about business and perseverance guided my responses during this chapter, **(Memories)**. My inclination to trust others, even when faced with red flags, stemmed from a foundational belief in giving people the benefit of the doubt—a trait instilled in me over the years, **(Beliefs)**. While this trust was tested, it ultimately revealed the importance of discernment and relying on God for wisdom in relationships, **(Biases)**.

Additionally, my wife's intuition played a significant subconscious role. Her hunch to check the PNC account was not random—it was a moment of divine prompting, emphasizing that God works through the instincts and insights of those closest to us, **(Motivations)**. The discovery of hidden funds was the culmination of both subconscious trust in her discernment and the unseen hand of God revealing the truth, **(Expectations)**.

Even the delay in transferring the deed can be seen as a subconscious alignment with God's timing. While I wasn't fully aware of why I didn't act sooner, it's clear that this pause was part of God's greater plan to bring about His purpose in a way that wouldn't have been possible otherwise, **(Assumptions)**. It's a powerful reminder that even our seemingly passive decisions can play a role in the divine orchestration of our lives.

INSIGHTFUL WISDOM

- **Relationships Are Reflections:** Every connection, whether harmonious or challenging, is divinely designed to shape you and prepare you for your purpose. Trust that even the most difficult relationships are part of God's plan.
- **Truth Will Be Revealed:** In God's timing, dishonesty and hidden motives come to light. This process, though painful, is necessary to align us with His truth and justice.
- **Faith Fuels Action:** Acting in faith, even when the outcome is unclear, positions you to walk in God's purpose. Every step taken in faith, whether bold or cautious, aligns with His greater plan.
- **Adversity Strengthens Character:** The trials we endure in relationships refine us. They teach us patience, resilience, and reliance on God, transforming us into the people He has called us to be.

A MOMENT TO REFLECT

- Can you identify a relationship that seemed challenging but ultimately shaped your character for the better?

- Have you witnessed God revealing truth or bringing clarity in a situation where you felt betrayed?
- Are you holding on to unresolved conflicts where God may be teaching you lessons of patience and discernment?

CONCLUSION: TRUSTING GOD IN EVERY CONNECTION

The experiences with David and Jeannie, though marked by conflict and challenges, were not random occurrences. Each event—the reconnection, the partnership, the betrayals—was intricately woven into God's greater plan. Through these moments, He revealed His timing, His justice, and His ability to use even painful situations for good.

Your relationships are no different. Whether they bring joy, hardship, or both, they are part of God's divine purpose for your life. Trust Him in the messiness, knowing that nothing is ever wasted. Every connection, trial, and triumph is a thread in the tapestry of His perfect plan. Life is not a coincidence; it's a masterpiece unfolding in His hands.

TAKE ACTION NOW!

A guide to navigating relationships with faith, discernment, and trust in God's timing.

1. TRUST GOD'S PURPOSE IN YOUR RELATIONSHIPS

Why: Every relationship, whether uplifting or challenging, serves a divine purpose. My bond with David began as mentorship and grew into a crucible for growth and discernment. Look at your relationships as tools God uses to prepare and refine you.

Result: Viewing relationships as part of God's divine design allows you to embrace both joys and challenges as opportunities for growth.

Scripture Reference: "By this everyone will know that you are my disciples, if you love one another." (John 13:35)

2. SEEK DISCERNMENT THROUGH PRAYER

Why: Relationships often bring challenges that require wisdom beyond human understanding. Pray for discernment as you navigate partnerships and conflicts, just as my wife's intuition led us to uncover hidden funds.

Result: Prayer opens your heart to God's guidance, helping you make decisions with clarity and wisdom.

Scripture Reference: "But the wisdom that comes from heaven is first of all pure; then peace-loving, considerate, submissive, full of mercy and good fruit, impartial and sincere.." (James 1:3)

3. ACT WITH INTEGRITY WHEN FACING INJUSTICE

Why: Confront dishonesty with grace and persistence, trusting that God will bring truth to light. Filing a claim against Jeannie wasn't easy, but standing for what was right aligned with God's principles of justice.

Result: Acting with integrity honors God and positions you for vindication in His timing.

Scripture Reference: "He has shown you, O mortal, what is good. And what does the Lord require of you? To act justly and to love mercy and to walk humbly with your God." (Micah 6:8)

4. EMBRACE DELAYS AS GOD'S TIMING

Why: Missed opportunities, like my delay in transferring the deed, are often part of God's greater plan. Trust His timing, knowing He is aligning events for His purpose.

Result: Trusting God's timing fosters patience and confidence in His sovereignty.

Scripture Reference: "But those who hope in the Lord will renew their strength. They will soar on wings like eagles; they will run and not grow weary, they will walk and not be faint." (Isaiah 40:31)

5. REMEMBER THAT TRUTH PREVAILS

Why: Dishonesty, no matter how deeply hidden, will eventually come to light. The discovery of financial discrepancies in my partnership with Jeannie reminded me of God's promise to reveal the truth in His time.

Result: Trusting God's justice strengthens your faith and reinforces your commitment to truth.

Scripture Reference: "But if we walk in the light, as he is in the light, we have fellowship with one another, and the blood of Jesus, his Son, purifies us from all sin." (1 John 1:7)

6. VALUE THE INPUT OF TRUSTED VOICES

Why: God often uses the intuition and wisdom of those closest to us. My wife's intuition to check the forgotten PNC account was a divine prompting that changed the course of events.

Result: Listening to godly counsel protects you from missteps and aligns your actions with wisdom.

Scripture Reference: "But whoever listens to me will live in safety and be at ease, without fear of harm." (Proverbs 1:33)

7. FOCUS ON GROWTH THROUGH CONFLICT

Why: Even difficult relationships are opportunities for refinement.

The challenges with David and Jeannie taught me patience, perseverance, and trust in God's justice. Let every trial build your character.

Result: Facing trials with faith and endurance produces spiritual maturity and resilience.

Scripture Reference: "Consider it pure joy, my brothers and sisters, whenever you face trials of many kinds, because you know that the testing of your faith produces perseverance." (James 1:2-3)

8. ACT WITH FAITH, EVEN IN UNCERTAINTY

Why: Taking deliberate actions, such as forming the partnership and later confronting financial misconduct, required faith. Trust that each step aligns with God's broader plan.

Result: Acting with faith unlocks opportunities for God to work through your efforts.

Scripture Reference: "Commit to the Lord whatever you do, and he will establish your plans." (Proverbs 16:3)

9. LET GO OF RESENTMENT AND SEEK RECONNECTION

Why: Relationships marked by conflict may still hold the potential for healing. My reconnection with David, though strained, demonstrated how God uses time to bring resolution.

Result: Forgiveness brings peace and opens the door for restored connections.

Scripture Reference: "For if you forgive other people when they sin against you, your heavenly Father will also forgive you." (Matthew 6:14)

10. TRUST THAT NOTHING IS WASTED

Why: Every challenge and triumph in your relationships is part of God's intentional design. The lessons I learned through conflict and partnership prepared me for future opportunities.

Result: Recognizing God's hand in every situation fosters trust and prepares you for His purposes.

Scripture Reference: "And we know that in all things God works for the good of those who love him, who have been called according to his purpose." (Romans 8:28)

Each relationship—whether a source of joy or tension—is part of God's intentional design to shape your character and prepare you for His plans. Trust that the challenges you face are refining tools, and the connections you form are threads in God's larger tapestry. As you navigate these relationships, trust that His hand is at work, aligning every step with His divine purpose. Nothing is wasted, and no encounter is a coincidence—it's all part of His greater plan.

Chapter 13
Divine Promises and the Return to the Property

MOVING ON

My Story #13: In 2012, my wife and I decided to leave the property and purchase a house in the same area. The constant struggles with Jeannie and David had become too much to bear, draining us emotionally and spiritually. It was clear that our family needed a fresh start, a place where peace could be restored.

From 2016 to 2024, David and I had little contact. The only exception came in 2019, a brief, chance meeting outside a PNC Bank. I saw him heading inside as I was leaving. Wanting to break the ice, I said, "Hey man, I still have the same feelings about you. You've known me since I was eighteen, and I learned so much from you." He nodded, acknowledging my words, and we went our separate ways. At the time, I didn't realize that God was quietly at work, weaving together the threads of a promise He had made years earlier.

THE PROMISE THAT NEVER LEFT

Despite the conflicts and challenges I had faced with Jeannie and David, I couldn't shake the words Jeannie had spoken to me in 2009: *"Allen, I want you to have this property."* It felt less like a casual statement and more like a divine declaration, echoing a promise I had sensed in my spirit for years.

That same year, I created a poster that still hangs on my wall today. It reads: *"Christian Believers Church: The Land Is Yours,*

Debt-Free, Pennsylvania. God Said It!" For over a decade, that poster has served as a daily reminder of the vision God placed in my heart. Even when circumstances seemed to contradict the promise, I clung to my faith, believing that God's word never returns void.

THE SANCTUARY PRAYER AND PROPHECY

In 2010, during a particularly trying time on the property, I felt overwhelmed by frustration and confusion. Turning to my wife, I said, "I don't know what God is doing here, but I'm going to the highest point on the property to pray."

She teased me, saying, "Who do you think you are? Moses!"

Her joke wasn't lost on me. Like Moses ascending Mount Sinai, I climbed to the highest point of the property, determined to seek God's guidance. But as I began to pray, a sudden downpour forced me to retreat to the sanctuary.

Sitting in the quiet of the sanctuary and after praying about my situation I pondered on what I should read in my bible. It was at that moment I thought about the joke my wife said about Moses. So I decided to read the book of Exodus as a result. While reading and in chapter 3 of Exodus, my phone rang. It was my uncle and bishop, calling unexpectedly. I didn't answer, choosing instead to focus on completing the book.

I decided to listen to his voice message when I reached Chapter 7. He left his new phone number, which I jotted down in the margins of Exodus Chapter 7 and continued to read.

When I completed the book I gave him a call back and he asked me how everything was going. I shared my frustrations about the property, and then my uncle asked me, "Do you have your Bible with you?"

"Yes," I replied.

He Said "Turn to the book of Exodus Chapter 3,".

I froze. It was the exact chapter where I was at when he initially called. The alignment was undeniable, a clear sign that God was orchestrating this moment.

My uncle then asked me to read verses 21-22, which recount God's promise to the Israelites: "And I will cause the Egyptians to look favorably on you. They will give you gifts when you go so you will not leave empty-handed." I read the passage aloud, and he explained, "Allen, you don't have to worry about this property. Just as God caused the Egyptians to release their wealth to His people, anyone who tries to hinder what God has planned for you will be powerless. You will not leave this situation empty-handed."

His words echoed the promise I had already felt stirring in my spirit. As I reflected on the chain of events—My wife's joke about Moses, the inspiration to read Exodus, the timing of my uncle's call, and his specific direction to this passage—I knew this wasn't a coincidence. God's hand was guiding every step, weaving these moments together to reaffirm His plan for me.

His words reaffirmed the promise I had already felt in my spirit. Despite the challenges, I knew God's hand was guiding every step.

THE UNEXPECTED RETURN

In January 2024, as I worked on a section of one of my books about mentors, I found myself reflecting on David. For two weeks, his name stayed on my mind. The thought of reconnecting with him weighed heavily, especially after learning that Tyler G. Hicks, another influential mentor in my life, had passed away. I regretted not being able to share with Tyler how much his guidance had meant to me. This spurred a sense of urgency about reaching out to David, even though our relationship had been strained.

Around the same time, my wife received a call from a friend who shared that David's son was telling people his father was sick and needed help. Feeling a deep prompting from God, I decided to check on David. Instead of heading home from Home Depot, I drove straight to the property.

When I arrived, I found David in the pool house. Unsure of how he would react after so many years, I approached cautiously. To my surprise, he greeted me warmly: "Hey son, how are you doing?"

We sat by the fireplace and talked for hours, reflecting on the past and catching up on everything that had happened since we last spoke. Then, David looked at me intently and asked, "Why are you here?"

Unsure of how to answer, I replied, "I don't know."

He asked again, "Why are you here?"

When I repeated, "I don't know, David. I just came to check on you," he asked a third time: "Why are you here?"

Finally, he said, "I know why you are here. You are here to buy the property."

At first, I dismissed the idea. But as his words lingered, I began to wonder if this was God's way of reigniting the promise He had made years earlier.

CHALLENGES AND OPPORTUNITIES

From that day forward, David and I communicated regularly. He shared that the retreat center was struggling, generating only a few thousand dollars a month. He admitted he was tired, lacked the strength to manage the property, and was ready to let it go.

I saw an opportunity to help him while also fulfilling what I believed was God's promise. I proposed a plan to revamp the business, increase revenue, and prepare the property for a potential purchase. Over the next eight months, I worked diligently, raising monthly income from $2,000 to $32,000 by improving marketing, redesigning the website, and attracting new customers.

However, despite my efforts, David reverted to old patterns. After working tirelessly for eight months to build up the property and increase its revenue, I asked for the money he owed me from our agreement. Instead of honoring his commitment, David refused to pay and began to dispute the arrangement. His actions, which included nickel-and-diming me throughout the process, left me no choice but to pursue legal action for the thousands of dollars I was rightfully owed. This betrayal resurfaced painful memories of my experiences with Jeannie and further strained our relationship.

In addition to the financial dispute, I had entered into a sales contract with David, intending to purchase the property. However, he interfered with the process, preventing the sale from being finalized. Although the sales contract has since expired, I retained the first right of refusal, giving me 30 days to match any legitimate offer and secure the property if it goes on the market. As I navigate this new chapter, I hold onto the scripture my uncle shared with me years ago. Like the Israelites, I trust that God will fulfill His promise in His perfect timing. Nothing about this journey has been a coincidence—it's all part of His divine plan.

THE 3 PILLAR PERSPECTIVE AT WORK

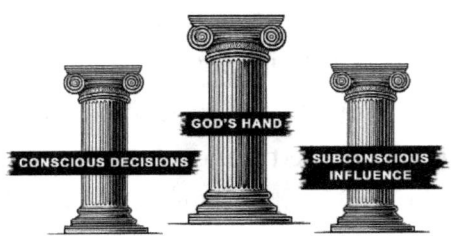

Pillar 1 - God's Divine Hand

God's hand is evident throughout this chapter, orchestrating events in ways that defy coincidence, **(Sovereignty)**. From Jeannie's original promise in 2009 giving me the property, to the scripture in Exodus revealed during a moment of prayer, God's fingerprints are all over this journey, **(Guidance)**. My uncle's phone call while I was immersed in the story of Moses in the book of Exodus chapter 3, and his guidance to read Exodus 3:21-22 when I called him back , further affirmed the divine nature of the promise, **(Intervention)**.

Even the timing of my reconnection with David in January 2024 highlights God's intricate planning, **(Timing)**. For weeks, David weighed heavily on my mind as I reflected on mentors in my life. Learning of Tyler G. Hicks' passing prompted a wave of reflection, and soon after, a phone call from my wife revealed a potential health crisis involving David. These seemingly unconnected events aligned perfectly to guide me back to the property at just the right moment, **(Favor)**. David's question—repeated three times—culminating in "You are here to buy the property," was another sign of God's sovereignty, pointing to a greater purpose unfolding in His timing, **(Provision)**.

Pillar 2 - Conscious Decisions

My conscious decisions played a critical role in responding to the opportunities and challenges God presented. When David refused to honor the financial agreements we had made after eight months of work, I had to make the difficult choice to pursue legal action, **(Accountability)**. It wasn't an easy decision, but it was necessary to stand up for what was right and ensure I wasn't taken advantage of, **(Responsibility)**. Similarly, entering into the sales contract with David showed my proactive approach in pursuing the property, even when obstacles arose, **(Discipline)**.

Another deliberate choice was my continued effort to restore the retreat center's operations despite past betrayals. By improving marketing, redesigning the website, and increasing revenue, I demonstrated resilience and faithfulness to the vision God placed in my heart, **(Intentionality)**. Even when the contract expired and David's actions became more difficult to navigate, I consciously chose to hold onto my first right of refusal and keep faith in the promise of ownership, **(Focus)**. These intentional steps reflect how aligning actions with faith is essential for seeing God's plans come to fruition, **(Risk)**.

Pillar 3 - Subconscious Influences

God often works through our subconscious instincts, preparing us in ways we don't fully understand at the time. My decision to immerse myself in scripture during a challenging moment on the property, and the seemingly random act of writing my uncle's number in the margins of Exodus 3, underscore how God was guiding me on a deeper level, **(Memories)**. Little did I know that the very chapter I had been drawn to would become the foundation of the prophecy spoken over my life, **(Beliefs)**.

Reflecting on David's question—"Why are you here?"—I see how God had been preparing me all along for the moment he declared, "You are here to buy the property." The poster I created in 2009, proclaiming "The Land Is Yours, Debt-Free," was a subconscious declaration of faith in God's promise, **(Expectations)**. Over the years, this daily reminder reinforced my belief in a future that seemed uncertain at times. God's subtle influences in my life ensured I stayed aligned with His purpose, even when I couldn't fully see the path ahead, **(Motivations)**.

INSIGHTFUL WISDOM

- **God's Promises Are Unshakable:** No matter how much time passes, God's word remains true. Trust that His plans are always in motion, even when circumstances seem to delay or deter the outcome.

- **Obedience Opens Doors:** Simple acts of faith and obedience—like showing up, seeking guidance in scripture, or honoring your commitments—can have far-reaching impacts that align you with God's will.

- **Preparation Happens in the Subconscious:** God often works through our thoughts, instincts, and habits, setting the stage for His purpose without us realizing it. What may seem like small, insignificant moments are often part of His greater design.

A MOMENT TO REFLECT

- Are there promises God has made in your life that seem delayed or forgotten?
- How has God's hand been evident in the relationships or opportunities He's placed before you?

- What subconscious patterns or habits might be shaping your decisions today, aligning you with His purpose?

CONCLUSION

Looking back, it's clear that every moment—every sanctuary prayer, every conversation, and even every conflict—has been part of God's divine plan. The property's reappearance in my life is no coincidence. From Jeannie's prophetic words to David's confirmations about the property, God has been orchestrating this journey for His glory.

While the outcome remains uncertain, I trust that God's promises never fail. This is more than a story about a piece of land; it's a testament to the power of faith, obedience, and the undeniable truth that nothing in life is random. Every event, every delay, and every trial is a step closer to His perfect plan.

TAKE ACTION NOW!

A guide to embracing divine promises and trusting God's timing through challenges and opportunities.

1. ANCHOR YOURSELF IN GOD'S PROMISES

Why: No matter how long it takes, trust that God's word will not return void. His promises are unshakable and will come to pass in His perfect timing. Like Jeannie's words in 2009 and the prophecy shared by my uncle, God's declarations over your life are eternal.

Result: Trusting in God's promises brings peace and assurance that His timing is always perfect.

Scripture Reference: "So is my word that goes out from my mouth: It will not return to me empty, but will accomplish what I desire and achieve the purpose for which I sent it." (Isaiah 55:11)

2. SEEK CLARITY THROUGH SCRIPTURE

Why: In times of uncertainty or frustration, turn to God's word for direction. My prayer in the sanctuary led me to Exodus 3, where God reaffirmed His plan. Scripture is often the channel through which God speaks directly to your circumstances.

Result: God's word illuminates your path and strengthens your faith as you navigate challenges.

Scripture Reference: "Your word is a lamp for my feet, a light on my path." (Psalm 119:105)

3. ACT ON DIVINE NUDGES

Why: When God prompts you to reconnect, explore an opportunity, or take a bold step, act in faith. My decision to visit David was spurred by a sense of urgency I couldn't ignore. God uses these nudges to align us with His will.

Result: Acting on divine guidance opens doors to new opportunities and blessings.

Scripture Reference: "In all your ways submit to Him, and He will make your paths straight." (Proverbs 3:6)

4. REMAIN FAITHFUL DURING DELAYS

Why: Delays are not denials. God's timing is often different from ours, but it is always perfect. Trust that what may seem like a setback is part of a larger plan to prepare you for what's ahead.

Result: Patience in God's timing leads to a deeper trust in His purpose.

Scripture Reference: "But those who hope in the Lord will renew their strength. They will soar on wings like eagles; they will run and not grow weary, they will walk and not be faint." (Isaiah 40:31)

5. BE OPEN TO NEW BEGINNINGS

Why: Reconnecting with David was unexpected, but it reopened the door to a promise God had made years earlier. Sometimes, what seems closed may simply be waiting for God's timing to reopen.

Result: Being open to God's plans allows for restoration and fulfillment of His promises.

Scripture Reference: "Being confident of this, that He who began a good work in you will carry it on to completion until the day of Christ Jesus." (Philippians 1:6)

6. STAND FIRM FOR WHAT IS RIGHT

Why: When faced with opposition or injustice, take a stand while remaining aligned with God's principles. Legal action against David wasn't an easy choice, but it was necessary to uphold integrity and justice.

Result: Standing for truth and justice aligns your actions with God's righteousness.

Scripture Reference: "He has shown you, O mortal, what is good. And what does the Lord require of you? To act justly and to love mercy and to walk humbly with your God." (Micah 6:8)

7. RECOGNIZE DIVINE PATTERNS IN YOUR LIFE

Why: Reflect on how God has been preparing you through past experiences, relationships, and challenges. My poster proclaiming "The Land Is Yours" was a subconscious declaration of God's promise. Recognize the signs He has placed along your path.

Result: Recognizing God's patterns builds faith and reveals His purpose in your life.

Scripture Reference: "Because of the Lord's great love we are not consumed, for His compassions never fail. They are new every morning; great is your faithfulness." (Lamentations 3:22-23)

8. PERSIST IN THE FACE OF CHALLENGES

Why: Obstacles often precede breakthroughs. Whether it's financial disputes or strained relationships, trust that God is working through the difficulty to fulfill His promise.

Result: Perseverance through trials leads to spiritual growth and eventual victory.

Scripture Reference: "Blessed is the one who perseveres under trial because, having stood the test, that person will receive the crown of life that the Lord has promised to those who love Him." (James 1:12)

9. REFLECT ON GOD'S FAITHFULNESS

Why: Look back at the ways God has shown up in your life. This will strengthen your faith as you await the fulfillment of His promises. Like the sanctuary prayer and my uncle's prophetic words, God's faithfulness is evident when we reflect.

Result: Remembering God's works inspires confidence in His continued faithfulness.

Scripture Reference: "I will remember the deeds of the Lord; yes, I will remember Your miracles of long ago." (Psalm 77:11)

10. STAY PREPARED FOR THE FULFILLMENT OF HIS PLANS

Why: Keep yourself aligned with God's purpose so you're ready when His promises come to fruition. Holding onto the first right of refusal for the property shows the importance of being positioned for what's next.

Result: Preparation ensures you're ready to step into God's promises when the time is right.

Scripture Reference: "See, I have placed before you an open door that no one can shut." (Revelation 3:8)

The challenges and promises in this chapter reveal that God's timing is always perfect. The strained relationships, missed opportunities, and delays weren't setbacks—they were setups for His greater plan.

For you, the promises God has spoken over your life are just as certain. Trust that every delay and every challenge is part of His intricate design. Your persistence, faith, and alignment with His will are bringing you closer to the fulfillment of those promises.

Remember: nothing in your life is random or coincidental—it is all part of God's divine purpose.

Chapter 14
Your Life is not a Coincidence

As I reflect on my journey at the age of 50, the divine alignment that has guided my life becomes undeniably clear. From the highs to the lows, from the moments of clarity to the times of confusion, God's hand has been present in every detail. It's not just a comforting thought—it's a profound truth. Before I even entered this world, before I was formed in my mother's womb, God had a plan for me, just as He does for you. As the prophet Jeremiah reminds us in **Jeremiah 1:5, *"Before I formed you in the womb I knew you, before you were born I set you apart; I appointed you as a prophet to the nations."*** This speaks to the intentionality of God in every life.

Everything in my life, from where I was born to the people I've encountered, has been orchestrated with purpose. The pain, the joy, the setbacks, and the triumphs have all worked together to create a legacy—a legacy that isn't just about me, but about how God's plan unfolds in each of our lives. It's all been part of a divine strategy, and through it all, I've come to one undeniable conclusion: *There are no coincidences.*

ALL THINGS WORK TOGETHER FOR GOOD

In Romans 8:28, the Bible declares, *"And we know that in all things God works for the good of those who love him, who have been called according to his purpose."* This verse has been a cornerstone of my faith. When we truly grasp the depth of "all things," we realize that it encompasses every single detail of our lives—good, bad, and in-between. It's a reminder that God is always at work, even when we can't see it.

Wisdom is essential to understanding this. As **Proverbs 4:7 says, *"Wisdom is the principal thing; therefore get wisdom: and with all thy getting get understanding."*** Understanding isn't just surface-level knowledge; it's the ability to discern God's movements in our lives, to recognize His hand in the details, and to trust His timing.

True understanding means seeing the bigger picture. It means comprehending how God uses time, events, and relationships to shape us into who we are meant to be. It's about realizing that the waiting, the preparation, and the in-between moments are just as important as the fulfillment of His promises.

THE IMPORTANCE OF TIME AND PREPARATION

God operates outside of time, while we live within it. To Him, everything is already complete, yet we experience His plan as a process. This process, though sometimes uncomfortable, is where the true work happens. It's where God refines us, teaches us, and prepares us for the blessings He's already ordained.

Think about this: God may promise you something today, but that doesn't mean it will manifest immediately. Why? Because He's preparing you to sustain the blessing. He's ensuring that you're ready for the weight of the purpose He has for you. The waiting period is not wasted time; it's development time. It's where character is built, faith is strengthened, and understanding is deepened.

Looking back on my own life, I can see how God used time to prepare me. From my early days of ministry to my business endeavors, to the challenges and victories with the property, every

162

step was intentional. At the moment, some of it didn't make sense. But as I look back, I see how God was working all things together for my good.

Your Life Is Not a Coincidence

If there's one truth I hope this book conveys, it's that your life is not a coincidence. Every moment, every encounter, and every challenge has a purpose. God has placed this book in your hands for a reason. Perhaps it's to remind you of a promise He made, to encourage you in a difficult season, or to help you see the divine alignment in your own life.

Consider this: Why are you reading this book at this particular moment? It's not random. It's part of God's plan for your journey. He wants you to understand that everything happening in your life is intentional. The people you meet, the situations you face, and even the obstacles in your path are all part of His strategy to shape you and fulfill His purpose in your life.

INSIGHTFUL WISDOM

As we close this chapter, I want to leave you with some principles to carry with you:

1. **God's Timing Is Perfect**
   Trust that His promises will come to pass at the right time. The waiting period is not a delay; it's preparation.

2. **Your Journey Is Unique**
   Don't compare your path to anyone else's. God's plan for you is tailor-made, and every step is intentional.

3. **Learn from Every Season**
   Every experience, whether joyful or painful, has a lesson. Embrace the process and grow through it.

> 4. **Faith Requires Action**
>
> Trusting God doesn't mean being passive. Take steps of faith, even when the outcome isn't clear.
>
> **Celebrate Small Victories**
>
> Recognize and celebrate the milestones along the way. They're reminders of God's faithfulness.

A CALL TO ACTION

I encourage you to take some time to reflect on your own life. Think about the moments that seemed random or insignificant. Can you see how God was working in those moments? What lessons have you learned? What promises are you holding onto?

Ask yourself:

- Where has God's hand been evident in my life?
- What steps can I take to align myself with His purpose?
- How can I trust His timing more fully?

A LEGACY OF PURPOSE

As I write this, I'm reminded that my life is not just about me. It's about the legacy I'm building for my family, my community, and those who will come after me. It's about fulfilling God's purpose and leaving a mark that points others to Him.

Your life has the same potential. You were created for a purpose, and everything you've experienced has been part of God's plan to prepare you for it. Trust Him. Lean into the process. And know that your legacy is being built with every step you take.

As the prophet Jeremiah wrote in **Jeremiah 29:11,** *"For I know the plans I have for you," declares the Lord, "plans to prosper you and not to harm you, plans to give you hope and a* *future."* Hold onto this promise. Believe that your life is not a coincidence. It's a masterpiece in progress, created by the hands of the Master Himself.

Go forth with confidence, knowing that God is with you, guiding you, and using every moment to fulfill His purpose in your life.

Bonus Chapter
Recognizing God's Hand Through the Three Pillar Perspective

I chose to include this bonus chapter to share additional ways God's hand works in our lives through the lens of the *3 Pillar Perspective*. This perspective highlights how divinity, conscious decisions, and subconscious influences shape the events we encounter daily. By revisiting these principles, I hope to show you real-life examples of how God's presence is unmistakable in guiding, protecting, and providing for us—even in ways we might not immediately recognize. These stories reaffirm the idea that life's events are not random but divinely orchestrated, urging us to trust His process fully.

1. DIVINITY: THE SUPERNATURAL ALIGNMENT OF EVENTS THAT COULD ONLY BE ORCHESTRATED BY GOD.

Divinity shines when something unexplainable occurs, defying human logic or effort. For example, consider the moment I met my wife. At a time when marriage was the furthest thing from my mind, our paths crossed in a way so serendipitous that it couldn't have been random. Within days, we were engaged, and over two decades later, I can look back and see how this divine alignment shaped every aspect of my life. God's divinity shows us that nothing happens by chance; it is His deliberate hand, steering events toward a greater purpose.

2. SOVEREIGNTY: GOD'S ABSOLUTE CONTROL OVER ALL CIRCUMSTANCES.

Sovereignty is God's ability to rule over every detail, no matter how small. In my life, this was evident when I was betrayed by close friends in business. While I initially questioned why God allowed it, those betrayals opened doors to new opportunities and relationships that I would have missed otherwise. Looking back, it's clear that God was always in control, ensuring that every setback was simply a setup for something greater.

3. FAVOR: UNEARNED BLESSINGS THAT POSITION YOU FOR SUCCESS.

Favor is when doors open that you didn't knock on or blessings come without your striving. When I was 18, I left a barbershop to work elsewhere, only to discover that my departure led the original shop owner to default on the lease in less than six months. This unexpected turn resulted in me becoming the shop owner, a role I wasn't pursuing but one that laid the foundation for my future success. Favor reminds us that what the world calls luck is often God's way of positioning us for blessings beyond our efforts.

4. PROTECTION: MOMENTS WHEN GOD SHIELDS YOU FROM HARM, OFTEN WITHOUT YOU REALIZING IT.

Protection can be seen in the near misses or dangers you never knew were looming. One day, while driving to pick up my wife from her grandmother's house in Brooklyn, I had my three sons in the back seat. I turned onto a street where the traffic light at the end of the block was green. Driving at about 30 mph, I inexplicably slowed down to 5 mph midway through the block. I questioned why I did so, but as I approached the intersection, a Lexus SUV sped through the red light on the cross street, narrowly missing my car. To this day, I believe God caused me to slow down, sparing my children and me from what could have been a devastating accident.

5. PROVISION: RESOURCES AND OPPORTUNITIES THAT COME WHEN YOU NEED THEM MOST.

My wife and I own a commercial building with an annual tax bill of $40,000. We had set aside $27,000 for this purpose, planning to gather the remaining $13,000 in the coming months. Unexpected expenses arose, shifting the normal plans to cover the balance.

As the tax deadline approached, a tenant in our building experienced a major plumbing issue—a toilet overflowed, causing water damage to their unit, the two units below, and the first-floor storefront. The insurance adjuster assessed the damage at around $22,000. After paying $6,000 to the mitigation company, we received $15,000 from the insurance company.

Since I'm familiar with contracting work, I handled the repairs myself, spending only $2,000 on materials. This left us with approximately $13,000—the amount needed to complete our tax payment. This wasn't luck; it was God's provision at work, ensuring we had exactly what we needed when we needed it.

6. GUIDANCE: GOD'S DIRECTION THROUGH CIRCUMSTANCES, PEOPLE, OR INNER CONVICTION.

Guidance often comes as a quiet nudge or a clear sign. When I decided to move my family to Pennsylvania to help with the retreat center, the choice wasn't easy. Prayer and unexpected confirmations—through scripture and conversations—gave me the clarity to move forward. Even when the full picture wasn't clear, God's guidance illuminated the path one step at a time.

7. INTERVENTION: WHEN GOD STEPS IN TO CHANGE THE COURSE OF EVENTS FOR HIS PURPOSE.

Intervention is when God disrupts the natural order to fulfill His will. One example is my encounter with the police. I didn't plan for my phone to capture incriminating audio evidence while confiscated, nor could I have predicted my wife's Spirit-led intuition to investigate financial records during a retreat business dispute. Both instances led to favorable outcomes in legal battles. These divine interventions turned the tide in ways I couldn't have orchestrated myself, reaffirming that God steps in to ensure His plans prevail.

8. TIMING: THE PERFECTION OF WHEN AND HOW EVENTS UNFOLD IN YOUR LIFE.

Timing is one of the most profound expressions of God's hand. In January 2024, I set a goal to write a book every month and designed the covers, including *Your Life Is Not a Coincidence.* I displayed these covers on my office wall for motivation and also posted them on Facebook as my cover image, intending to write this particular book sooner.

The spark to start came when my mother's friend, Carolyn Battle, saw the book cover on Facebook and asked her, "When will the *Your Life Is Not a Coincidence* book be available?" When my mother shared this with me, I felt an immediate urgency to begin writing.

That same weekend, a series of unexpected events further confirmed God's timing. While driving to New York from Pennsylvania on Friday, my car hydroplaned, crashing into another vehicle and the guardrail. Thankfully, I was unharmed, but the insurance company deemed the car totaled, relieving me of the financial burden of repairs and interest. The crash required me to stay in New York longer than planned.

On Saturday, I attempted to pick up a rental car from Enterprise, but complications with the staff delayed the process. They informed me I wouldn't be able to get a car until Monday, forcing me to stay at my mother's house through Sunday. This delay, which might seem like an inconvenience, was clearly part of God's orchestration.

On Saturday evening, I shared with my mother about the series of events surrounding the car accident and my work on this book. During that conversation, she mentioned how it would have been nice for me to preach at her church the next day. However, she told me that Reverend Marie was scheduled to deliver the sermon, so I dismissed the thought, even though I felt that God had given me a message from John 9.

On Sunday morning, shortly before the service began, Reverend Marie fell ill and was unable to preach. My mother informed the pastor that I was in town, and he invited me to speak with only about 20 minutes' notice. I delivered a message titled *Your Life Is Not a Coincidence,* sharing how every event, even those that seem random, is divinely orchestrated.

That message wasn't just for the congregation; it reaffirmed for me that this book had to be written. Within a week, I completed the manuscript, reflecting on how God's perfect timing aligns everything in our life.

These events were not coincidental; they were God's way of showing me the importance of trusting His timing in all things.

LIVING WITH THE THREE PILLAR PERSPECTIVE

This bonus chapter was written to give you deeper insight into how God's hand moves in your life, often in ways we don't initially see. The Three Pillar Perspective is a framework for understanding how **God's Hand**, your **Conscious Decisions**, and **Subconscious Influences** work together to shape your experiences and lead you toward His purpose. By recognizing these patterns, you can better navigate life's challenges, embrace its blessings, and trust in the divine timing of it all.

As I conclude this book, I want to introduce you to the journey ahead. My next book, *The Problem Is You,* will focus on the third pillar—Subconscious Influences—and explore how these hidden patterns often work against us. It will challenge you to look inward, take accountability, and overcome the habits that keep you from progress. The subconscious is one of the enemy's most effective tools, keeping us blind to the recurring issues that block our growth. This book will empower you to identify, confront, and break free from those strongholds.

The Three Pillar Perspective is about equipping you to live with clarity, confidence, and purpose. By applying these principles, you can see the miraculous in the mundane, the purpose in the pain, and the opportunities in the obstacles. Remember, your life is not a coincidence—it is part of God's intentional plan. Trust Him, and take each step in faith as He continues to lead you into the fullness of His design for your life.

Exercise #1
Subconscious Transformation: Reprogramming Your Mind

The objective of this exercise is for you to intentionally reprogram your subconscious with affirmations and intentional thought patterns. God has given you the power to renew your mind and transform your habits through His Word and affirmations of faith. By repeating affirmations, you align your beliefs with God's purpose and position yourself to live a life of divine fulfillment.

INSTRUCTIONS:

1. **Speak these affirmations aloud daily:**
   - Choose a consistent time each day, such as in the morning or before bed.
   - Speak each affirmation with conviction and belief.
2. **Visualize God's promises as you speak:** Imagine living out these truths, walking boldly in faith, and experiencing breakthroughs.
3. **Write your affirmations:** Take a moment to create a few personal affirmations that resonate deeply with you. Record them below and refer to them regularly.

FOR EXAMPLE:

Here are a few affirmations for you to begin with:

- "I am aligned with God's purpose for my life." **(Alignment, Sovereignty)**

- "I trust in God's timing and His plan for my future." **(Timing, Guidance)**
- "My past does not define me; I walk in God's provision and grace." **(Provision, Memories)**

Now it's your turn! Write down three affirmations that reflect God's promises and your personal journey.

Exercise #2
Reflection Journaling: Aligning Your Thoughts

The purpose of this exercise is for you to reflect on your journey, align your thoughts with God's purpose, and recognize the divine setups in your life. Journaling creates a space for clarity, growth, and revelation.

INSTRUCTIONS:

1. **Set aside time for reflection**: Choose a quiet place where you can write without distractions.
2. **Answer thought-provoking prompts**: Use the prompts below to guide your reflections.
3. **Write your answers**: Record your reflections and revisit them over time to see how God is moving in your life.

FOR EXAMPLE:

Here are reflection prompts to guide your journaling:

- What moment in your life seemed like a coincidence but turned out to be a divine setup? *(Sovereignty, Intervention)*
- What subconscious beliefs or habits might be holding you back, and how can you realign them? *(Beliefs, Habits)*
- How have God's favor and provision shown up in your life, even when you didn't expect them? *(Favor, Provision)*

Take time now to write your thoughts for one or more of the prompts above. Use the space below for your reflections.

Exercise #3
Meditative Prayer: Be Still and Know

This exercise is for you to connect with God on a deeper level through meditative prayer, combining scripture, stillness, and intentionality to align your heart and mind with His purpose.

INSTRUCTIONS:

1. **Find a quiet space**: Sit comfortably and close your eyes.
2. **Breathe deeply**: Take slow breaths to center yourself.
3. **Meditate on a scripture**: Choose one of the following verses and repeat it slowly, letting the words resonate in your spirit.
4. **Write your thoughts and prayers**: After meditating, write down what God reveals to you during this time.

FOR EXAMPLE:

Scriptures for meditation:

- *"Be still and know that I am God."* (Psalm 46:10) ***(Focus, Guidance)***
- *"For I know the plans I have for you,"* declares the Lord. (Jeremiah 29:11) ***(Timing, Sovereignty)***
- *"The Lord is my shepherd; I lack nothing."* (Psalm 23:1) ***(Provision, Favor)***

Reflect on these scriptures. What did you hear, feel, or realize during your meditative prayer? Write your thoughts below.

_____

_____

Exercise #4
Breaking Habits:
Overcoming Barriers

The objective of this exercise is for you to identify habits that no longer serve your purpose and replace them with new, intentional patterns aligned with God's will. With God's guidance, you can break free from the subconscious cycles that keep you stuck and step into His promises.

INSTRUCTIONS:

1. **Identify a habit to break**: Write down one habit or pattern that hinders your growth.
2. **Explore the root cause**: Reflect on the subconscious beliefs, fears, or motivations driving this habit.
3. **Replace it with intentional action**: Write a new habit or practice that aligns with God's purpose for you.
4. **Pray for strength**: Ask God to give you the discipline to break free and embrace the new habit.

FOR EXAMPLE:

- **Habit to Break:** Procrastination *(Fears, Biases)*
- **Root Cause**: Fear of failure or perfectionism.
- **New Habit:** Begin tasks immediately and celebrate progress, not perfection *(Intentionality, Discipline)*.

Now, take time to reflect on your own habits. Write down the habit you want to change, its root cause, and the intentional action you will take to overcome it.

Exercise #5
Speaking Life:
Affirmations of Faith

This exercise is for you to declare life-giving affirmations over yourself daily, reinforcing your identity in Christ and aligning your subconscious with His promises. Speaking life transforms how you see yourself and the world around you.

INSTRUCTIONS:

1. **Choose affirmations to speak aloud**: Use the examples provided or create your own.

2. **Repeat them daily**: Speak them with confidence and conviction.

3. **Personalize your declarations**: Write affirmations specific to your journey and purpose.

FOR EXAMPLE:

Affirmations to Speak:

- *"I am fearfully and wonderfully made."* (Psalm 139:14) *(Beliefs, Favor)*
- *"I walk in God's provision and protection daily."* *(Provision, Protection)*
- *"God's timing is perfect, and I trust His plan for my life."* *(Timing, Guidance)*

Write your personalized affirmations here and commit to speaking them daily.

Exercise #6
Vision Mapping:
Aligning Goals with Purpose

The goal of this exercise is for you to create a vision map that aligns your life goals with God's purpose. By writing down your vision and making it plain, you step into intentionality and focus, positioning yourself to fulfill His promises.

INSTRUCTIONS:

1. **Set your vision**: Write down one goal or dream God has placed on your heart.
2. **Break it into actionable steps**: Identify the steps needed to achieve it.
3. **Reflect on alignment**: Ensure your goals align with God's purpose for your life.
4. **Pray over your vision**: Dedicate it to God and ask for His guidance and favor.

FOR EXAMPLE:

- **Vision:** Start a business that serves the community *(Intentionality, Guidance).*
- **Steps**:
    1. Research the market.
    2. Write a business plan.
    3. Seek mentorship and resources. *(Accountability, Discipline)*
- **Prayer:** *"Lord, align my dreams with Your will and guide my steps as I pursue this vision."*

Now, write down your vision, break it into steps, and dedicate it to God in prayer. Use the space below to plan your next steps.

Exercise #7
Daily Gratitude Practice: Seeing God in the Small Things

The purpose of this exercise is for you to cultivate gratitude, recognizing God's provision and favor in every area of your life. Gratitude shifts your perspective and deepens your trust in God's sovereignty.

INSTRUCTIONS:

1. **Set aside time daily**: Reflect on moments where you see God's hand in your life.
2. **Write three things you're grateful for each day**: Focus on both big and small blessings.
3. **Thank God in prayer**: Use this time to acknowledge His provision and faithfulness.

FOR EXAMPLE:

Gratitude List:

- God's protection during a challenging day *(Protection, Sovereignty)*.
- A kind word from a friend that uplifted my spirit *(Favor)*.
- Progress on a personal goal, even if small *(Discipline)*.

Write your daily gratitude list here. Return to this space regularly to build a habit of gratitude.

_____

_____

_____

About the Author

Allen Brown is a lifelong minister and successful entrepreneur whose journey with Christ began on Easter morning in 1998, leading to a profound commitment to ministry in 1999. With over twenty-five years of experience in Christian ministry, Allen has dedicated his life to uplifting believers, spreading the gospel, and equipping others with practical tools to grow spiritually and succeed in life.

Married to his devoted wife, Melissa, for 27 years, Allen is the proud father of four young adult sons. Together, the Brown family has built a strong foundation centered on faith, family, and business. Allen's entrepreneurial journey began early in life—his first structured business at age 18 led to remarkable success, including generating millions of dollars in revenue and creating employment opportunities for many.

Currently, Allen focuses on his passion for writing and empowering others through *Build Our Kingdom Publishing*, a company dedicated to producing Christian-based books that inspire believers to align with God's purpose. As a published author of multiple transformative works, Allen shares wisdom drawn from his faith journey and entrepreneurial experiences to help individuals embrace their God-given potential.

In addition to his publishing work, Allen is an active public speaker and community leader. He delivers motivational and faith-based messages designed to encourage growth, resilience, and spiritual alignment. Through his outreach efforts, Allen continues to inspire communities, emphasizing the power of biblical principles to transform lives.

For more information about his books, speaking engagements, and ministry, visit **www.allenbrownministries.com**.

When not working on new projects, Allen enjoys spending quality time with Melissa and their sons. Together, they exemplify the values of love, perseverance, and service, reflecting Allen's unwavering commitment to glorifying the Lord and empowering believers to thrive in every aspect of life.

About Build Our Kingdom Publishing

BUILD OUR KINGDOM PUBLISHING

——— BUILD OUR KINGDOM.COM ———

WE ARE A CHRISTIAN BOOK PUBLISHER WITH THE FOCUS ON PUBLISHING NON-FICTION LITERATURE TO EDIFY AND BUILD THE KINGDOM OF GOD.

OUR VISION IS TO SEE PEOPLE COME TO JESUS CHRIST AS A RESULT OF THE TITLES WE RELEASE.

FOR MORE BOOKS BY ALLEN BROWN

VISIT BUILDOURKINGDOM.COM

Million Dollar Seed

How My Last $17,600
Grew to Millions God's Way

"Million Dollar Seed" tells the extraordinary journey of faith, obedience, and divine intervention that transformed the author's final $17,600 into a thriving financial and spiritual breakthrough. This inspiring narrative goes beyond material success, exploring the profound impact of trusting God's guidance in the face of uncertainty.

The author shares candid reflections on challenges that tested and strengthened his faith. Paralleling his experiences with biblical figures like Abraham, the story highlights the timeless principles of faith and obedience in unlocking God's blessings.

Structured around three pivotal phases—life before Christ, awakening faith, and a deep trust in God—the book provides a roadmap for spiritual growth and personal transformation. More than a financial success story, "Million Dollar Seed" reveals the deeper wealth found in peace, joy, and alignment with God's purpose.

A source of motivation and practical wisdom, this book invites readers to trust in God's plan, persevere through challenges, and embrace the limitless possibilities of divine guidance.

I Will Teach You How to Hear God's Voice

In a world filled with distractions, hearing God's voice can feel elusive. Yet, the opportunity to connect with the Divine is closer than you think.

In *I Will Teach You How to Hear God's Voice,* Allen Brown draws from his own profound experiences to illuminate the path to divine communication. Through compelling personal stories and biblical wisdom, Allen unveils the life-changing power of hearing and following God's voice in every area—family, business, finances, and ministry.

This guidebook dismantles doubts and affirms that God yearns to communicate with you, guiding you toward your unique purpose. Packed with practical exercises and spiritual insights, it equips readers to cultivate sensitivity to God's whispers, interpret His silence, and deepen trust and faith.

More than a book, this is an invitation to discover a relationship with God that transforms your life. Let His voice be your guiding light.

The Christian Entrepreneur's Compass Volume 1

33 Biblical Strategies for Growing Your Business

"The Christian Entrepreneur's Compass Volume 1" by Pastor Allen Brown offers 33 powerful strategies to help entrepreneurs align their businesses with biblical principles. Drawing from timeless lessons in Scripture, Pastor Brown highlights stories of figures like Isaac, Jacob, and Joseph, transforming their experiences into actionable insights for modern business challenges.

This guide provides a unique blend of faith and practicality, encouraging readers to balance profit with purpose while building ethical, God-centered businesses. Each chapter delivers wisdom and tools to navigate today's marketplace with integrity and spiritual growth at the forefront.

Perfect for entrepreneurs, leaders, and professionals seeking to integrate their faith into their work, this book serves as a roadmap to lasting success. Whether starting a new venture or enhancing an existing one, "The Christian Entrepreneur's Compass Volume 1" inspires readers to achieve business goals while fulfilling their divine purpose.

Escape the Rat Race: God's Way

ESCAPE THE RAT RACE
GOD'S WAY

DISCOVER BIBLICAL SECRETS THAT CAN
UNLOCK YOUR PATH TO FINANCIAL FREEDOM

Pastor Allen Brown

"Escape the Rat Race: God's Way" reveals a divine path to financial freedom and spiritual abundance. This transformative guide combines biblical wisdom with practical financial insights, offering seven foundational principles— Faith, Obedience, Sacrifice, Wisdom, Resourcefulness, Gratitude, and Generosity— that lead to true prosperity as ordained by God.

More than a financial manual, this book is a roadmap to a life of purpose, fulfillment, and impact. Each chapter weaves practical advice with spiritual truths, making it accessible to anyone seeking a deeper understanding of wealth and success. It challenges conventional ideas of prosperity and invites readers to embrace spiritual richness alongside material abundance.

Whether trapped in the monotony of daily life or searching for greater meaning, "Escape the Rat Race: God's Way" inspires a shift in priorities. Experience wealth that transforms not just your bank account but your heart and spirit. Start your journey to lasting joy, peace, and divine prosperity today.

The Problem Is You
A Transformational Guide to Self-Discovery and Change

Have you ever felt stuck in your finances, career, relationships, or personal growth—wondering why success and happiness seem just out of reach? The truth might be hard to accept: the biggest obstacle in your life is often staring back at you in the mirror.

In *The Problem Is You*, you'll uncover the hidden beliefs, habits, fears, and assumptions—the **elements of subconscious influence**—that silently sabotage your progress. Through relatable stories, practical solutions, and powerful biblical insights, this book shows how these unseen forces shape every decision and outcome in your life.

With 101 problems divided into 24 easy-to-navigate categories, *The Problem Is You* helps you identify the blind spots holding you back and empowers you to take control of your success. Whether you're facing challenges in money, relationships, career, or self-worth, this book will equip you with tools to transform your mindset and achieve lasting change.

Your breakthrough starts here.

101 Relationship Problems That Steal Your Joy

101 Relationship Problems That Steal Your Joy offers a powerful guide to overcoming the challenges that hinder joy in your relationships. Whether you're single or in a relationship, this book addresses the problems that create emotional distance, dissatisfaction, and frustration. You'll uncover key issues, such as miscommunication, unrealistic expectations, unhealthy patterns, and the deep-rooted beliefs that prevent connection and happiness.

Each problem is explored through real-life examples, subconscious influences, and practical solutions you can start applying immediately. This book empowers you to break free from destructive cycles, build stronger connections, and foster deeper, more fulfilling relationships.

The complete guide provides valuable insights for both individuals and couples, offering actionable steps to reclaim happiness and create the love life you deserve. Don't let unresolved problems stand between you and your fulfillment. Start your journey toward a better, more joyful relationship today!

www.ingramcontent.com/pod-product-compliance
Lightning Source LLC
Chambersburg PA
CBHW060805120626
46557CB00001B/94